ZECHARIAH

A Study of the Prophetic Visions
of Zechariah

By

G. COLEMAN LUCK

MOODY PRESS
CHICAGO

CONTENTS

5

BACKGROUND

The Prophet

When the Bible student opens his Old Testament to the prophecy of Zechariah, he encounters the people of Israel at a most critical period of their history. Eighteen long years have now elapsed since Cyrus the Great conquered the Babylonian Empire (Zech. 1:1; Ezra 5:1; 4:24; 1:1). What a joyful time that had been for the Israelites! After seventy trying years of captivity in Babylon, at last they had been granted royal permission to return to their own land and rebuild their beloved capital city, Jerusalem (Ezra 1:2, 3). Many of them, however, had felt too firmly settled in Babylon to risk leaving that land for pioneer work; only a minority—a remnant—had returned under the leadership of Zerubbabel the governor and Joshua the high priest (Ezra 1:4-6). But this returning remnant was filled with burning enthusiasm. Within seven months' time they had rebuilt the sacred altar of burnt offering and were once more performing the sacrificial rites commanded by Jehovah in the Law of Moses (Ezra 3:1-6).

Not long after the beginning of the second year they had started to rebuild the temple itself. At that time the foundations of that noted structure were laid, and

7

probably the first course of stones (Ezra 3:8-13). But then, to their dismay, bitter opposition on the part of the Samaritans had developed—opposition that eventually succeeded in disrupting the work (Ezra 4:1-23). Finally, discouragement was complete, and no attempt was made to continue the construction of the temple or city walls.

Eventually the ruler who forbade the work was assassinated. Sad to say, the people then proved to be slack to take advantage of this opportunity. To spur them on, God raised up a great prophet—Haggai—with the very message so needed for that hour (Ezra 5:1-2; Hag. 1:1; cf. Zech. 1:1). Haggai's principal ministry was evidently that of exhorting the people to rebuild the temple (Hag. 1:2, 4, 8; 2:3-4). To this end he delivered four short but striking messages which are recorded in his small book in the Old Testament.

His exhortation brought about a revival. Just in the midst of this revival, God raised up still another prophet to give further messages to the people. The name of this prophet was Zechariah (cf. Hag. 1:1; 2:1; Zech 1:1). The name is a very common one in the Old Testament (used of at least twenty-seven other people) and means "one whom Jehovah remembers." It is clear that Zechariah was a very young man at the time he delivered his message to the people and wrote the book now bearing his name. In 2:4 he is called a "young man." This represents the same Hebrew word used by Saul in speaking of David in I Samuel 17:33, and by Jeremiah of himself in Jeremiah 1:6. Since Zechariah wrote in the second year of Darius (Zech. 1:1)—commonly called "Darius Hystaspes"—which we know was eighteen years after the first year of Cyrus' rule in Babylon (the time of the return to Jerusalem), it is evident that Zechariah must have been brought back from Babylon to Canaan at a very early age—doubtless while just a small boy.

What other facts are known concerning this prophet? Investigation shows that he is also mentioned in Ezra 5:1; 6:14; and Nehemiah 12:4, 16. From these verses we learn that his grandfather Iddo was a priest. Since his father Berechiah is not mentioned in these references, it is thought that he must have died at an early age, so that Zechariah later succeeded his grandfather in the priestly office. As to his later life, nothing is revealed in the Bible. According to Jewish tradition he was a member of the Great Synagogue, a council originated by Nehemiah and composed of 120 members. Ezra is said to have been the president of this council, which was later succeeded by the well-known Sanhedrin. Other traditions indicate that Zechariah lived to a great age and was finally buried at Jerusalem by the side of his fellow prophet, Haggai.[1] However another account states that he suffered death by martyrdom.

THE BOOK

Our principal concern in the present study is not Zechariah himself, but rather the book he wrote. It is one of three postexilic prophetic writings of the Old Testament. It is undoubtedly one of the least known books of the Bible and has often in the past been considered very difficult of interpretation, perhaps because of the visions given. However, "these difficult passages

[1]Arno C. Gaebelein, *The Annotated Bible*, V, 263.

are readily interpreted in the light of the whole body of related prophecy."[2]

As already indicated, Zechariah began his prophetic office two months after Haggai (cf. Hag. 1:1; Zech. 1:1). He was a companion prophet of Haggai and was used of God to encourage the people in rebuilding the Temple and the city. However, Zechariah's message seems to be more in the nature of encouragement than of rebuke, as was the case with Haggai. "The difference between the two prophets seems to be this, that while Haggai's task was chiefly to rouse the people to the outward task of building the Temple, Zechariah took up the prophetic labors just where Haggai had left it, and sought to lead the people to a complete *spiritual* change, one of the fruits of which would of necessity be increased zeal in the building of God's House, the completion of which he witnessed four years later."[3]

To us today Zechariah's book is of great and significant interest because of the wide range of prophecy contained in it. Both advents of Christ are presented. The future of Israel is revealed. Prophecy is also given concerning Gentile world powers. "Zechariah was the great unveiler, the man through whose message the people were enabled to see things which, while actual, were nevertheless obscured by the prevalent conditions of adversity. . . . These men were looking at the near; Zechariah bade them look through to the things beyond."[4] His book has been called "the Apocalypse of the Old

---

[2]C. I. Scofield, *The Scofield Reference Bible,* p. 965.
[3]David Baron, *Visions and Prophecies of Zechariah,* p. 9.
[4]G. Campbell Morgan, *Living Messages of the Books of the Bible,* p. 319.

Testament." *Apocalypse* means "unveiling," "the removal of something that hides."

Zechariah's book is not difficult to read. "Graphic
vividness is his peculiar merit."[5] The date of the writing
of this book can with certainty be set at 520-518 B.C. The
key word, "LORD of hosts," is used fifty-two times. This
expression is found no less than eighteen times in one
chapter—chapter 8. As to the book itself, after a brief
introduction we find a series of ten visions recorded in
the opening six chapters. These are "not easy of exposi-
sion, but flaming with light, singing in hope, and res-
onant in confidence."[6] Chapters 7-8 contain a certain
question asked of Jehovah, and the answer of the Lord
to that question. Then in the last six chapters (9-14) is
found the marvelous picture of a great Saviour-King who
shall first suffer and later reign, bringing wonderful blessing to Israel and to the whole world. The final chapters
also contain many details concerning the last days before
the return of Christ.

[5]Robert Jamieson, A. R. Fausset, and David Brown, *A Commentary on the Old and New Testaments*, III: XLVII.
[6]Morgan, p. 318.

THE OUTLINE

III. THE DOWNFALL OF THE NATIONS AND THE
SALVATION OF ISRAEL (9:1–14:21)
- A. The Burden of Hadrach (9:1-8)
- B. The Coming King and the Deliverance He Will
Bring to Israel (9:9-17)
- C. Blessing for Judah and Ephraim (10:1-12)
- D. The True Shepherd Rejected for the False Shepherd
(11:1-17)
- E. The Siege of Jerusalem and the Deliverance of
Jehovah (12:1-14)
- F. The Cleansing of Israel (13:1-6)
- G. Scattering of Israel After the Shepherd Is Smitten
(13:7-9)
- H. The Coming King and the Kingdom (14:1-21)

1

PROPHETIC VISIONS
(1:1—6:15)

THE INTRODUCTION (1:1-6)

IN THE EIGHTH MONTH, in the second year of Darius,
came the word of the LORD unto Zechariah, the son
of Berechiah, the son of Iddo the prophet, saying,
The LORD hath been sore displeased with your
fathers (1:1-2).

Though the human author is Zechariah, the real Author
is revealed in the expression "the word of the LORD." As
in the case of other Bible books, here a very real claim
is made to divine inspiration.

When the meaning of Zechariah's name is combined
with that of his father's and his grandfather's, a beautiful
statement of truth is to be found. *Zechariah* means
"Jehovah remembers." *Berechiah* means "Jehovah
blesses"; while *Iddo* means "His time." The combined
thought would be "Jehovah remembers and Jehovah
blesses in His time."[1] This is surely a message of comfort
not only to Israel but to God's people of every age and
in every place.

[1]Arno C. Gaebelein, *The Annotated Bible*, V, 263.

The opening message from the Lord has to do with past times. Jehovah had been "sore displeased" with the ancestors of Zechariah's generation. The Hebrew is literally "displeased with displeasure," an expression that suggests no mild feeling but rather a very strong and vehement displeasure. The people well knew this to be true because of the judgments that had been sent on Israel, especially the destruction of Jerusalem by Nebuchadnezzar and the seventy years of captivity in Babylon. The reason for God's extreme displeasure is made clear in the words that soon follow.

"Therefore say thou unto them, Thus saith the LORD of hosts; Turn ye unto me, saith the LORD of hosts, and I will turn unto you, saith the LORD of hosts" (1:3). This in brief is the message of the Lord for the prophet's own generation. There had been revival, and the people had returned to the land of God's choice. Yet evidently they had not fully returned in a spiritual way to the Lord Jehovah. The great truth presented here surely applies in all ages—"turn ye unto me, saith the LORD of hosts, and I will turn unto you." James 4:8 tells us "draw nigh to God, and he will draw nigh to you." The writer of Hebrews (11:6) informs us that God "is a rewarder of them that diligently seek him."

After the gracious invitation a word of warning, of exhortation, is sounded:

> Be ye not as your fathers, unto whom the former prophets have cried, saying, Thus saith the LORD of hosts; Turn ye now from your evil ways, and from your evil doings: but they did not hear, nor hearken unto me, saith the LORD (1:4).

The people are warned not to be like their fathers—their hardhearted, unbelieving fathers. What a sad situation when children must be told not to emulate the ways of their parents, of their ancestors! Usually children do follow the example their fathers give them. Modern fathers and mothers should seriously consider whether their lives present an example to their children which the latter can safely follow or one against which they must be warned.

Let us carefully observe just what the evil example of the fathers consisted of—that against which the Israelites are so solemnly warned. First, they fell into evil ways, disobeying God's holy law. Then, when God in mercy sent prophets to warn them and to urge them to turn again to the Lord, they hardened their hearts, refusing to hear and hearken. "He, that being often reproved hardeneth his neck, shall suddenly be destroyed, and that without remedy" (Prov. 29:1).

After the warning comes a tremendous object lesson.

> Your fathers, where are they? And the prophets, do they live forever? But my words and my statutes, which I commanded my servants the prophets, did they not take hold of your fathers? And they returned and said, Like as the LORD of hosts thought to do unto us, according to our ways, and according to our doings, so hath he dealt with us (1:5-6).

The fathers, along with the prophets who warned them, are now gone from this earthly scene; but the Word of God which the prophets spoke has been completely fulfilled. His words and statutes "took hold of" (or "overtook") the fathers. Though men may seek to evade them, God's judgments are inexorable. "Be sure your sin will find you out" (Num. 32:23). Though God's messengers are but human, God's Word is eternal.

After the people of Israel had been carried away into Babylonian captivity, they acknowledged their sin, and God's justice in punishing it. But, oh, the sadness of the thought that their confession came too late to avoid the terrible reaping of their evil sowing! "Be not deceived; God is not mocked: for whatsoever a man soweth, that shall he also reap" (Gal. 6:7).

After this preparatory message Zechariah now passes to the record of the prophetic visions which were given him some three months later.

THE VISIONS OF ZECHARIAH (1:7—6:15)

Ten wonderful visions are now described. The usual procedure with regard to these visions is that the prophet is first shown something. Then, his curiosity being aroused, he asks a question concerning the thing seen. In response to this question an interpretation is provided.

1. *The Vision of the Horses and the Man Among the Myrtles* (1:7-17)

> Upon the four and twentieth day of the eleventh month, which is the month Sebat, in the second year of Darius, came the word of the LORD unto Zechariah, the son of Berechiah, the son of Iddo the prophet, saying, I saw by night, and behold a man riding upon a red horse, and he stood among the myrtle trees that were in the bottom; and behind him were there red horses, speckled, and white (1:7-8).

The date which is given shows that three months have

elapsed since the warning was given to the people not to follow in the footsteps of their fathers. It seems that all ten of the following visions were given in one night to the prophet—one after another in quick succession. The first of these visions very clearly speaks of judgment on the nations because of their too severe treatment of Israel. The visions themselves are called "the word of the LORD" and are thus placed on an equal basis with direct prophecy as being fully authoritative.

In this particular vision Zechariah saw *a man riding on a red horse.* As this man is said to be *standing* among the myrtle trees in the bottom, it is evident that he is mounted on the horse but at the present moment is stationary. Who is this horseman? It seems very clear from the context (1:11) that he is *the Angel of the Lord.* A careful study of this term in the Old Testament will reveal that it refers, not to an ordinary angel, but to the preincarnate Christ.[2] The horse on which this mighty One rides is *red,* this being the color that usually speaks of war and bloodshed.

The place where the Horseman is located is *among the myrtles.* The original Hebrew word used here is an interesting one. It is apparently the basis of the Hebrew name for Esther—*Hadassah* (Esther 2:7). The word speaks of the *myrtle tree*—a tree that is humble but fragrant. The expression *in the bottom* is rather difficult in the original language to translate. Scholars believe it to mean "a shady place," or "a deep place."[3] The position of this Rider no doubt speaks of the fragrance of Israel, so far as Jehovah is concerned, and the place of

[2]Gaebelein, *The Angels of God,* chap. 3.
[3]Jamieson, Fausset and Brown, IV, 661.

sorrow through which the chosen nation has just passed.
At this very time Israel was in a lowly and melancholy
condition, and humanly speaking there was little hope of
relief. But "man's extremity is God's opportunity."
They are soon to be shown that God is preparing to work
in a wonderful way for His people.

Behind this Rider there are also other horses. Some are
red, again symbolizing war and bloodshed; others are
white, the color which speaks of victory. Still others are
speckled (or bay, or roan colored). This apparently represents a combination of the other two colors.

Very naturally, the prophet's curiosity is aroused, and
he asks a question of an interpreting angel standing nearby. "Then said I, O my lord, what are these?" (1:9). He
does not ask *who* these are but *what.* He is desirous of
knowing the meaning and purpose of these horsemen.

"And the angel that talked with me said unto me, I
will show thee what these be" (1:9). Literally the expression is "the angel that spoke *in* me." "The very rare
expression seems to convey the thought of an inward
speaking, whereby the words should be borne directly
into the soul, without the intervention of the ordinary
outward organs."⁴ This interpreting angel promises to
show Zechariah "what these be."

The Man on the red horse now speaks and answers the
question put by the prophet to the interpreting angel.

> And the man that stood among the myrtle trees
> answered and said, These are they whom the LORD
> hath sent to walk to and fro through the earth
> (1:10).

⁴E. B. Pusey, *The Minor Prophets,* II, 342.

Just as Satan walks about the earth for evil (Job 1:7, 2:2; I Peter 5:8), so the Lord Jehovah has His representatives walking up and down in the earth to examine the affairs of men. This is indeed a solemn thought.

The other riders now make their report to the Angel of the Lord, who is identified as the One among the myrtles.

> And they answered the angel of the LORD that stood among the myrtle trees, and said, We have walked to and fro through the earth, and, behold, all the earth sitteth still, and is at rest (1:11).

Israel has been conquered and is in a stricken condition. Now the earth is at peace, but it is a peace that is not pleasing to God. There is such a thing as an unrighteous peace.

> Then the angel of the LORD answered and said, O LORD of hosts, how long wilt thou not have mercy on Jerusalem and on the cities of Judah, against which thou hast had indignation these threescore and ten years? (1:12).

In view of the supremacy of the Gentile nations and the stricken condition of Israel, the Angel of the Lord (the preincarnate Christ) speaks now to the Lord (the first Person of the Trinity) in intercession for Judah and Jerusalem. His words *how long* are both a question and an appeal. Seventy years of God's indignation are mentioned referring to the time of the Babylonian captivity. God had promised (Jer. 25:11-12) that the land would lie desolate for that length of time, but now the period

has been fulfilled and Jerusalem is still suffering. On
the other hand, Israel's enemies are at rest.

In reply the Lord Jehovah speaks directly to the interpreting angel who had talked with Zechariah, since
the answer is given for Zechariah's benefit, in order that
he may carry it to the people. "And the LORD answered
the angel that talked with me with good words and comfortable words" (1:13). Just what these good and comfortable words are the next four verses reveal.

> So the angel that communed with me said unto
> me, Cry thou, saying, Thus saith the LORD of hosts;
> I am jealous for Jerusalem and for Zion with a
> great jealousy. And I am sore displeased with the
> heathen that are at ease: for I was but a little dis-
> pleased, and they helped forward the affliction
> (1:14-15).

The interpreting angel now gives the "good words and
comfortable words" of Jehovah to Zechariah. He is told
to "cry thou": "The vision was not for the prophet alone.
What he saw and heard *that* he was to proclaim to others.
The vision, which he now saw alone, was to be the basis
and substance of his subsequent preaching, whereby he
was to encourage his people to persevere."[5]

When the Lord says, "I am jealous for Jerusalem," the
verb in the original language indicates a state entered in
the past and continuing on into the present. Even when
it did not seem so, the Lord Jehovah was and continues
now to be jealous for Jerusalem against the nations
plundering it. The contrasting side of Jehovah's jealousy
for Jerusalem is His anger with the nations—"I am sore

[5]*Ibid.*, p. 344.

displeased with the heathen." He was angry with Jerusalem for a little while and allowed the heathen nations to conquer and overthrow it. However, these nations, in giving vent to their wrath upon Jerusalem, have gone beyond that which was in the heart of God.

Because of this God says that He has again "returned to Jerusalem," that is, returned in the sense of once more visiting it with His wonderful mercies.

> Therefore thus saith the LORD; I am returned to Jerusalem with mercies: my house shall be built in it, saith the LORD of hosts, and a line shall be stretched forth upon Jerusalem (1:16).

God's *house* (the temple) shall again be built in it. The *line stretched forth* signifies immediate action is to be taken by God. Once before the line had been stretched for *immediate judgment* (II Kings 21:13). Now the line is again to be stretched—this time for *immediate blessing*.

The prophet is again commanded to give out his message to all the people of Israel.

> Cry yet, saying, Thus saith the LORD of hosts; My cities through prosperity shall yet be spread abroad; and the LORD shall yet comfort Zion, and shall yet choose Jerusalem (1:17).

The cities of the land of Israel, God's peculiar possession, "shall yet be spread abroad" (or overflow). Just as a fountain gushes forth and overflows, so shall God's people once again be spread over the land that had been desolate. Prosperity shall again be found in the land. Why? Because "the Lord shall yet comfort Zion, and shall yet choose Jerusalem."

No doubt there was a near fulfillment of this prophecy for the generation of Israelites to which Zechariah personally ministered. About four years later the temple was completed, and some time after that the city wall was rebuilt by Nehemiah. Further, and supremely, the Lord comforted Zion in a very real way by the sending of His Servant the Branch (3:8) —the Messiah—who came several hundred years later to "preach the gospel to the poor . . . to heal the brokenhearted, to preach deliverance to the captives, and recovering of sight to the blind, to set at liberty them that are bruised, to preach the acceptable year of the Lord" (Luke 4:18-19) .

But Israel as a nation rejected that Messiah (John 1:11) . And in the 1,900 long, dreary years that have followed Messiah's first coming, Israel has been in a dispersion, a captivity, far more trying than that in Babylon. Jerusalem was again desolated and since has been "trodden down of the Gentiles" (Luke 21:24) . Surely the prophecy of Zechariah 1:17 looks beyond the prophet's generation to that glorious day when the Lord Jesus (as prophesied in Amos 9:11-12 and quoted by James in Acts 15:16-17) says:

> After this I will return, and will build again the tabernacle of David, which is fallen down; and I will build again the ruins thereof, and I will set it up: that the residue of men might seek after the Lord, and all the Gentiles, upon whom my name is called, saith the Lord, who doeth all these things.

Remember however that before that great rebuilding there must intervene the present age of grace, an age largely unforeseen by the Old Testament prophets, an age (to quote once again from James in the verses just preceding those above referred to) in which God is visiting "the Gentiles, to take out of them a people for his name" (Acts 15:14).

So there will yet be a glorious day for Jerusalem and Zion, when the great Son of David returns to rule and to reign. Of that day the apostle Paul writes: "And so all Israel shall be saved: as it is written, There shall come out of Sion the Deliverer, and shall turn away ungodliness from Jacob: for this is my covenant unto them, when I shall take away their sins" (Rom. 11:26). In that day, "all their present sorrows [shall] not only be balanced, but forever silenced, by divine consolations."[6]

2. *The Vision of the Four Horns* (1:18-19)

Zechariah's second vision is now presented: "Then lifted I up mine eyes, and saw, and behold four horns" (1:18). "It seems as though at the close of each vision Zechariah sank in meditation on what had been shown him; from which he was aroused by the exhibition of another vision."[7] This time he sees *four horns*. The horn is often used in Scripture as the symbol of *power* and *authority,* the image being taken from the beast whose strength is in its horns. In addition this symbol sometimes includes the idea of *evil pride* as well as power. (For typical symbolical uses of the *horn* see Ps. 92:10; Dan. 7:8, 11, 20-21; etc.)

"And I said unto the angel that talked with me, What be these? And he answered me, These are the horns

[6]Matthew Henry, *Commentary on the Whole Bible,* IV, 1406.
[7]Pusey, p. 346.

which have scattered Judah, Israel, and Jerusalem"
(1:19). As he did with the first vision, the prophet asks
the interpreting angel to inform him as to the meaning
of this vision. Very likely these four horns represent the
four great world powers spoken of by Daniel: Babylon,
Media-Persia, Greece, and Rome. These great powers
have been instrumental in scattering Israel.

If the question be asked: "What comfort is there for
Israel in this vision?" the words of David Baron provide
an adequate answer:

> Though it may have been intended as an indica-
> tion to the prophet, and a forecast that the *final*
> deliverance of Israel, and the overthrow of Israel's
> foes, was, from the prophet's point of time, yet
> remote, the wonderful and consoling fact set forth
> in the vision remains; that in spite of all the great
> Gentile powers, who would each in turn take up
> the work of scattering and afflicting Israel, Israel
> would not be wholly swallowed up nor be over-
> whelmed, but would remain when all those powers
> should have disappeared, and would triumph in
> God's deliverance when the memory of their mighty
> enemies should be buried in shame and oblivion.
> . . . Israel is indestructible. The bush may burn,
> but it cannot be consumed, because God has said:
> 'Though I make a full end of all nations whither
> I have scattered thee, yet will I not make a full end
> of thee.'[8]

3. *The Vision of the Four Workmen* (1:20-21)

"And the Lord showed me four carpenters" (1:20).
The third vision is that of *four carpenters,* or *workmen.*

[8]David Baron, *Visions and Prophecies of Zechariah,* pp. 48, 51.

The original word used here means literally "workers in wood, stone, or metal."

> Then said I, What come these to do? And he spake, saying, These are the horns which have scattered Judah, so that no man did lift up his head: but these are come to fray them, to cast out the horns of the Gentiles, which lifted up their horn over the land of Judah to scatter it (1:21).

These *workmen* are evidently divine agents sent by God against the world powers. Just as the powers mentioned above have scattered Judah, so these four workmen (or *artificers*) are to "fray" or "terrify" the oppressing world powers. What are these four agents of God? It has been suggested that they may represent the four judgments of God mentioned in Ezekiel 14:21 and Revelation 6:1-8, these being war, famine, wild animals, and pestilence.[9] Another suggestion which seems more probable is that they represent four successive powers that overthrow the four empires pictured in the previous vision: that is, Media-Persia overthrew Babylon, Greece overthrew Media-Persia, Rome overthrew Greece, and the revived Roman Empire of the last days will be overthrown by the great Messianic kingdom.[10] Certainly the general truth is clearly brought out that every evil power that rises up against the people of God will eventually be overthrown and judged.

4. *The Vision of the Man with the Measuring Line* (2:1-13)

---

[9]C. I. Scofield, *Scofield Reference Bible*, p. 966.
[10]Baron, p. 53.

Once again a new vision is shown to the prophet.

> I lifted up mine eyes again, and looked, and be-
> hold a man with a measuring line in his hand.
> Then said I, Whither goest thou? And he said
> unto me, To measure Jerusalem, to see what is the
> breadth thereof, and what is the length thereof
> (2:1-2).

The symbol of the measuring line, suggested in 1:16,
is now used again. There the "line stretched forth"
spoke of blessing for Jerusalem, with God returning to
that city to comfort Zion. There was a near fulfillment
of the prophecy in the work of restoration done by Nehemiah. But the principal and complete fulfillment yet
awaits that future day when the Lord will indeed "return to Jerusalem" (1:16).

No doubt this vision is similar to that which Ezekiel
describes in 40:3. This is the same "man" who was seen
in Zechariah 1:8; this is "the man whose name is The
BRANCH" (6:12). In other words, this is the preincarnate second Person of the Trinity appearing here as the
Angel of Jehovah. In Ezekiel 40 He measures the city
for blessings it will yet enjoy in the glorious millennium.

Therefore we can say of Zechariah's present vision that
while it undoubtedly had a distinct local application—to
encourage the generation to whom Zechariah preached
with the thought that God was then going to bless them
—yet in its fullness the prophecy looks far beyond this
to the final regathering of Israel and the blessing to come
upon the land of Palestine during the millennium.

And, behold, the angel that talked with me went

forth, and another angel went out to meet him, and
said unto him, Run, speak to this young man, saying, Jerusalem shall be inhabited as towns without
walls for the multitude of men and cattle therein:
For I, saith the LORD, will be unto her a wall of fire
round about and will be the glory in the midst of
her (2:3-5).

After answering Zechariah's question, the interpreting
angel "goes forth" to speak to the Man with the measuring line and secure further information from Him
about the meaning of the symbol. But before he reaches
this Man (who is none other than our Lord, as already
seen) the Man with the measuring line sends back an
angel who is attending Him with the desired information.

This second angel tells the interpreting angel to "run,
speak to this young man," that is, to Zechariah. It must
be indeed a precious and important message since the
interpreting angel is commanded to *run* back to Zechariah with it. What is this message? That Jerusalem shall
yet "be inhabited as towns without walls for the multitude of men and cattle therein." In other words, though
the city is now in a depressed condition, days of marvelous prosperity yet lie ahead. Though the population is
now meager, yet some day it shall overflow from the city
so that no walls can hold it. For a further indication of
this condition Ezekiel 36:10 should be noted: "And I
will multiply men upon you, all the house of Israel, even
all of it: and the cities shall be inhabited, and the wastes
shall be builded."

But if the population far overflows the walls of the

city, then what will afford them protection against possible enemies? The answer given speaks of something even more wonderful than the promise of material prosperity: the city will not need any wall, because the Lord Jehovah Himself will be a wall of fire roundabout. More than that He will be "the glory in the midst of her." These expressions are quite reminiscent of the way in which the Lord Jehovah led His people through the wilderness to the promised land, with the Shekinah glory-cloud by day and the pillar of fire by night (Exodus 13:21).

Again the question must be asked: Have these promises yet been completely fulfilled? No, they have not. How foolish to say that such promises have been fulfilled in the blessing which God has granted the church in the present age! The city against which God had indignation (1:12) was certainly the literal city of Jerusalem. Surely the city He will bless in the manner just described is likewise the literal city of Jerusalem. Someday Israel's Messiah (and the Christian's Saviour) will come again to fulfill these wonderful promises. In that day the name of the city will indeed be "Jehovah-Shammah"—"The Lord is there" (Ezek. 48:35). Immanuel—"God in the flesh"—will be there as "the glory in the midst of her!"

> Ho, ho, come forth, and flee from the land of the
> north, saith the LORD: for I have spread you abroad
> as the four winds of the heaven, saith the LORD.
> Deliver thyself, O Zion, that dwellest with the
> daughter of Babylon (2:6-7).

A solemn warning is now given to the children of Israel still remaining there to flee from "the land of the north,"

which speaks of Babylon. The Lord formerly spread
them abroad "as the four winds of the heavens," but
now He calls on them to return. Many of the Israelites
had settled down in Babylon and in the other countries
to which they had been dispersed, and had failed to avail
themselves of the opportunity to return to their own
land. Now such are warned to return, not only because
of the blessings God is going to grant to Jerusalem, but
also because judgment is about to fall upon Babylon and
troublous times are in store for those who dwell there.[11]

Again it must be said that this return from Babylon
during the days of Zechariah was but a foreshadowing
of the final regathering of Israel preparatory to the wonderful earthly reign of their Messiah.

> And it shall come to pass in that day, that the
> Lord shall set his hand again the second time to re-
> cover the remnant of his people, which shall be
> left, from Assyria, and from Egypt, and from
> Pathros, and from Cush, and from Elam, and from
> Shinar, and from Hamath, and from the islands of
> the sea. And he shall set up an ensign for the na-
> tions, and shall assemble the outcasts of Israel, and
> gather together the dispersed of Judah from the
> four corners of the earth (Isa. 11:11-12).

Jeremiah likewise speaks of this great future regathering:

> And I will gather the remnant of my flock out of
> all countries whither I have driven them, and will
> bring them again to their folds; and they shall be

[11]History records that Babylon revolted twice during Darius' reign
and was twice reconquered. The first revolt seems to have occurred
around the time Zechariah was ministering, the second some six years
later. Both occasions were times of terrible suffering.

fruitful and increase. And I will set up shepherds
over them which shall feed them: and they shall
fear no more, nor be dismayed, neither shall they
be lacking, saith the LORD. Behold, the days come,
saith the LORD, that I will raise unto David a righteous Branch, and a King shall reign and prosper,
and shall execute judgment and justice in the
earth. In his days Judah shall be saved, and Israel
shall dwell safely: and this is his name whereby he
shall be called, THE LORD OUR RIGHTEOUS-
NESS. Therefore, behold, the days come, saith the
LORD, that they shall no more say, The LORD liveth,
which brought up the children of Israel out of
the land of Egypt; but, The LORD liveth, which
brought up and which led the seed of the house of
Israel out of the north country, and from all countries whither I had driven them; and they shall
dwell in their own land (Jer. 23:3-8).

Following this warning, there are some wonderful
Messianic verses:

For thus saith the LORD of hosts; After the glory
hath he sent me unto the nations which spoiled
you: for he that toucheth you toucheth the apple
of his eye. For, behold, I will shake mine hand
upon them, and they shall be a spoil to their servants: and ye shall know that the LORD of hosts hath
sent me. Sing and rejoice, O daughter of Zion: for,
lo, I come, and I will dwell in the midst of thee,
saith the LORD. And many nations shall be joined
to the LORD in that day, and shall be my people:
and I will dwell in the midst of thee, and thou
shalt know that the LORD of hosts hath sent me
unto thee. And the LORD shall inherit Judah his

portion in the holy land, and shall choose Jerusalem again (2:8-12).

The words of verse 8 present a strange mystery. This
verse states that the Lord (Jehovah) of hosts says: "He
hath sent me." The question naturally arises, Who would
have the power to send the Lord Himself? The answer
is found in verse 9: "The LORD [Jehovah] of hosts hath
sent me." But with this answer the mystery deepens, and
apparently is greater than ever, for the Scripture actually
says that "the Lord sent the Lord," or "Jehovah sent
Jehovah." Those who accept the Old Testament but reject the New have a mystery here which is absolutely in-
soluble. How can Jehovah send Jehovah?

How clear, however, the matter becomes in the light
of the New Testament! The first Person of the Trinity
sends the second Person. The Father sends the Son;
thus Jehovah (the first Person) sends Jehovah (the second Person). The One sent is the great Messiah, and
the reference absolutely proves His deity and equality
with the Father. Exactly the same One speaks here who
speaks in Isaiah 61:1:

> The Spirit of the Lord GOD is upon me; because
> the LORD hath anointed me to preach good tidings
> unto the meek; he hath sent me to bind up the
> brokenhearted, to proclaim liberty to the captives,
> and the opening of the prison to them that are
> bound.

This verse Jesus Christ definitely stated was fulfilled in
Himself (Luke 4:16-21).

Again it must be admitted that there may well be a

local application of the statement in the sending of the
preincarnate Christ (as the Angel of Jehovah) against
the nations at that time, but surely the prophecy chiefly
looks to the far future—to the day of the Lord, for it is
affirmed that this sending shall take place "after the
glory." The expression refers to the glorious second
coming of Christ, at which time He will save Israel and
then bring the Gentile nations into judgment (Matt.
25:31-46).

The dearness of Israel to God is shown in the expression that one touching her is touching "the apple of his
eye." "For the LORD's portion is his people; Jacob is the
lot of his inheritance. He found him in a desert land,
and in the waste howling wilderness; he led him about,
he instructed him, he kept him as the apple of his eye"
(Deut. 32:9-10). The "apple" refers to the eyeball, or
pupil of the eye. "The pupil, or aperture, through which
rays pass to the retina, is the tenderest part of the eye;
the member which we most sedulously guard from hurt,
as being the dearest of our members; the one which
feels most acutely the slightest injury, and the loss of
which is irreparable."[12] God must love Israel a great
deal to describe the nation in this way. If God loves this
nation so much, all true Christians should likewise love
Israel and seek her good. God's continuing love for this
nation even in its unbelief is forcefully affirmed in Romans 11:28-29.

In that future day of consummation, these nations that
have plundered Israel are to become plunder to them
who have been their servants. How blessed to know that

[12]Jamieson, Fausset and Brown, IV, p. 665.

then Israel shall know "that the LORD of hosts hath sent" the Son (2:9)!

Verse 10 gives a preview of the millennial joy of Israel when all these glorious prophecies have come to pass. Israel is called upon to be in great joy because of the blessings, for they have been restored to their land, and Jehovah (their Messiah, the Lord Jesus Christ) dwells in the midst of them. Here, "Lo, I come" refers *not* to the *first* coming of the Messiah, when, as Daniel says, "shall Messiah be cut off, but not for himself" (Dan. 9:26), and as Isaiah says, "he shall be cut off out of the land of the living" when He "shalt make his soul an offering for sin" (Isa. 53:10). This "Lo, I come" refers to the *second* advent of Christ, the blessed hope yet ahead.

The blessings of the millennium, when the Lord Jesus Christ is reigning on earth, are pictured in verses 11 and 12. The joy then will not be for Israel alone but "many nations shall be joined to the Lord in that day." God is going to dwell on earth in the person of Immanuel. Then will Israel know indeed that the Lord Jesus Christ is their true Messiah—"thou shalt know that the LORD of hosts hath sent me unto thee." As for the Lord's side of the picture, verse 12 states that at last He will inherit Judah for His portion in the Holy Land.

The chapter closes with a call to all nations to be silent before the Lord. "Be silent, O all flesh, before the LORD: for he is raised up out of his holy habitation" (2:13). The expression that God is "raised up out of his holy habitation" simply means that, though God seemed to be slumbering, it is clear at least that He is watching over His people.

5. *The Vision of the Clothing of Joshua, the High Priest (3:1-10)*

In this fifth vision Zechariah is shown Joshua, the high priest. From other Scripture references we find that this man Joshua was the high priest at the time of the return of the Jews from their captivity in Babylon, some sixteen years before this (see Ezra 4:3; 5:2; Hag. 1:1, 12; 2:2; Zech. 6:11-15).

In this particular vision Joshua is seen as the high priest, and thus as the representative of his people Israel, "standing before the angel of the Lord." The latter personage has already been shown to be an appearance of the Son of God *before* His earthly incarnation. *This vision does not have reference to Joshua's personal character.* It is not Joshua the *man* standing before the Lord, but Joshua the *high priest*, who has entered the holy of holies to appear before God for his nation. Up to this time the visions have spoken of the outward circumstances of Israel, the blessings God will pour out upon them, and the judgment upon their enemies. But the question may well arise as to how He can do such things for a sinful nation. The present vision answers that question. There will be an inner change. God will cleanse the nation. So the removal of the filthy garments and the placing of the clean raiment on Joshua depicts that which Jehovah will do for the nation Israel.

At the same time, in a secondary application, a beautiful gospel picture can also be seen in this vision. This scene illustrates the way in which Christ is the believer's Advocate before the Father (I John 2:1). It also shows how the sinner's filthy rags of righteousness are exchanged for the pure linen of the righteousness of God through Christ. Considered in this light, the passage shows (1) the condition of the sinner "clothed with filthy garments" (v. 3; cf. Isa. 64:6; Prov. 30:12; Jude 23; Rev. 7:14); (2) Satan's opposition (v. 1) as he stands at the sinner's right hand to resist Him (God); (3) God's election—His sovereign choice—"the Lord hath chosen" (v. 2); (4) salvation itself, as God plucks the brand out of the fire (v. 2—*Joshua* means "Jehovah saves"); (5) the glorious transformation of sinner to saint (vv. 4-5); (6) subsequent service to God on the part of the redeemed one (vv. 6-7).

But now to return to the primary application of God's redeeming work for the nation Israel. "And he showed me Joshua the high priest standing before the angel of the LORD, and Satan standing at his right hand to resist him" (3:1). Israel's high priest is standing before the Lord on behalf of his people, but another character is also standing there—Satan, that great and evil resister of God. Here is an enlightening view of this wicked being in his position as adversary or accuser (cf. Job 1-2; Rev. 12:10). Satan, once the great archangel of God, fell through pride but is still permitted to enter into God's presence to make his accusations.

What a dramatic picture! Into the holy of holies comes Israel's high priest to appear for his nation. Will God accept or reject his ministrations? Satan appears, "to be Satan." His resistance is not just to Israel but to

God Himself.   He argues that God cannot receive such
sinful people—that He must reject Joshua and his people, for He is a holy God. "The scene is therefore a
judicial one. . . . [Satan] comes forward here as the enemy
and accuser of Joshua, to accuse him in his capacity of
high priest."[13]

Although Satan actually had no basis on which to
accuse Job, he does in this instance have some reality
behind his complaint against Joshua. This official had
permitted the people to cease their building of the temple, and Israel itself was contaminated with sin.

But, thank God that when this "prosecuting attorney"
makes his charge, there is a "defense attorney," an Advocate, to answer.

> And the LORD said unto Satan, The LORD rebuke
> thee, O Satan; even the LORD that hath chosen
> Jerusalem rebuke thee: is not this a brand plucked
> out of the fire? (3:2) .

These words are incomprehensible unless it is recognized that there is more than one Person in the Godhead,
for this verse states that "the LORD [Jehovah] said unto
Satan, The LORD [Jehovah] rebuke thee, O Satan." This
statement is repeated for emphasis. Here as in Psalm 110
the second Person (the Son) speaks to the first Person
(the Father) . The rebuke is similar to that administered
by Michael the archangel as recorded in Jude 9. How
wonderful to know that God's people have an Advocate,
a Mediator who is Himself divine! How wonderful to
know that God Himself is our Advocate (see Rom. 8:31-
33) !

[13]C. F. Keil, *The Twelve Minor Prophets*, II, 251.

Satan's charge is spurned and God's blessing of Israel
is justified on three grounds: (1) His sovereign choice
and election—"the Lord hath chosen Jerusalem"; (2) Israel's suffering for their sin, so that the nation is compared with a charred stick that has barely been rescued
from complete destruction in the fire—"Is not this a
brand plucked out of the fire?" (cf. Isa. 40:1-2) ; (3)
God will cleanse them. This is stated a bit later in verse
9—"I will remove the iniquity of that land in one day."
The fulfillment of this prophecy is yet to take place.
When will this day be?

> And I will pour upon the house of David, and
> upon the inhabitants of Jerusalem, the spirit of
> grace and of supplication; and they shall look unto
> me whom they have pierced; and they shall mourn
> for him, as one mourneth for his only son, and shall
> be in bitterness for him, as one that is in bitterness
> for his first-born (Zech. 12:10, ASV) .

This statement affirms that some day they will look unto
God whom they have pierced. This could only refer to
the death of their Messiah. When they do this "in that
day there shall be a fountain opened to the house of
David and to the inhabitants of Jerusalem for sin and
uncleanness" (Zech. 13:1) . That fountain is opened
now to every individual who will look in faith to the
pierced One.

Thus is it demonstrated that Israel, represented by
Joshua, is to be acquitted because Jehovah has chosen
them and him, and has pledged His love to them. The
picture is an apt one. Israel has indeed suffered severe
punishment and remains as a brand snatched from the

fire (Amos 4:11), largely consumed and yet miraculous-
ly preserved.

"Now Joshua was clothed with filthy garments, and
stood before the angel" (3:3). The garments Joshua
has on are described as "filthy." These speak of the
defilement of sin (see Isa. 64:6; 4:3-4; Prov. 30:12).
Satan has been rebuked now, and the scene changes from
a judicial one to a picture of cleansing from the defilement of sin.

> And he answered and spake unto those that stood
> before him, saying, Take away the filthy garments
> from him. And unto him he said, Behold, I have
> caused thine iniquity to pass from thee, and I will
> clothe thee with change of raiment (3:4).

The Angel of Jehovah speaks to angels standing nearby
and commands that the filthy garments be removed from
Joshua. This is not done by Joshua himself. The Lord
then tells Joshua, the representative of the people, that
his iniquity has been caused to pass from him. Not only
is this true, but he is also to be clothed in "a change of
raiment." The word here literally refers to festal (or
rich) apparel. Thus not only is sin to be removed, but
a gift of righteousness is to be given, represented by this
fine clothing. This suggests the "garments of salvation
and pure robe of Messiah's own perfect righteousness, in
which Israel shall then be attired."[14] This is none other
than the imputed righteousness of God given now to
the believer in the Lord Jesus Christ (Rom. 3-4).

After this scene, the prophet is moved to make a
petition. "And I said, Let them set a fair miter upon

14Baron, p. 98.

his head. So they set a fair miter upon his head, and clothed him with garments. And the angel of the LORD stood by" (3:5). Zechariah asks that a "fair miter" be placed on the head of Joshua. *Miter* is the word used for the headdress of a king or a prince. It is possible that here it speaks of the coming king of Israel, who would be the nation's chief glory. The request of the prophet is immediately granted.

> And the angel of the LORD protested unto Joshua, saying, Thus saith the LORD of hosts; If thou wilt walk in my ways, and if thou wilt keep my charge, then thou shalt also judge my house, and shalt also keep my courts, and I will give thee places to walk among these that stand by (3:6-7).

The Angel of Jehovah now protests or testifies. This means He calls God to witness. It is evident a solemn charge is about to be given to Joshua. This solemn charge is to the effect that if the priests will live for the Lord, both in their personal lives and in their official acts, they will be granted the privilege of judging the house of God. They are also given the responsibility of keeping the courts of God in a pure condition, and it is promised to them that they will have a place of access into the presence of God.

> Thus applied to the future, the sense of the whole verse would be this: "If thou wilt walk in My ways and keep My charge, thou shalt not only have the honor of judging My house, and keeping My courts, but when thy work on earth is done thou shalt be transplanted to higher service in Heaven, and have places to walk among these pure angelic

beings who stand by Me, harkening unto the voice of My word" .(Ps. 103:20, 21). Note the "if's" in this verse, my dear reader, and lay to heart the fact that, while pardon and justification are the free gifts of God to all that are of faith, having their source wholly in His infinite and sovereign grace, and quite apart from work or merit on the part of man, the honor and privilege of acceptable service and future reward are conditional on our obedience and faithfulness: therefore seek by His grace and in the power of His Spirit to "walk in his ways and to keep his charge," and in *all things,* even if thine be the lot of a "porter" or "doorkeeper" in the House of God, to present thyself approved unto Him, in remembrance of the day when "we must all be manifested before the judgment seat of Christ, that each one may receive the things done in the body, according to what he hath done, whether it be good or bad" (II Cor. 5:10) .[15]

"Hear now, O Joshua the high priest, thou, and thy fellows that sit before thee: for they are men wondered at: for, behold, I will bring forth my servant the BRANCH" (3:8). Joshua is now commanded to pay particular heed to what is to follow, together with the other priests who serve under him. These Old Testament priests are said to be "men wondered at," or literally, "men of a sign." They are a sign in the sense that they are a type of the great Priest who is to come—the Lord Jesus Christ—the Messiah of whom God said: "Thou art a priest forever" (Ps. 110:4). Then a great prophecy of this coming High Priest is given. He is here called by God, "my servant the BRANCH." (This name is also

[15]*Ibid.,* p. 105.

used in Isa. 11:1; Jer. 23:15; Zech. 6:12, and is one of the titles of Christ.) The term speaks, among other things, of the Messiah's fruitfulness and of the fact that He will come from the stock of Israel.

In Old Testament prophecy this title "the Branch" is used of the Messiah in four principal ways. Each of these four ways corresponds to an aspect of Christ's character emphasized in one of the Four Gospels of the New Testament: (1) Messiah is called "a Branch of *David*" (Isa. 11:1; Jer. 23:5; 33:15). This speaks of His being the rightful promised *King* of Israel. The gospel of Matthew clearly shows the fulfillment of this prophecy. (2) Messiah is called by God "my *servant* the BRANCH" (3:8). The gospel of Mark presents the Messiah—the Lord Jesus—as the suffering Servant of the Lord, obedient even unto death. (3) Messiah is called "the *man* whose name is The BRANCH" (6:12-13). Luke's gospel pictures Christ as the perfect Man—the only perfect and sinless man who has ever lived. (4) Messiah is called "the branch of Jehovah" (Isa. 4:2, ASV), speaking of His Immanuel character, of the fact that He is "God with us." John's gospel in a marvelous way emphasizes this feature of His wonderful person.

> For behold the stone that I have laid before Joshua; upon one stone shall be seven eyes: behold, I will engrave the graving thereof, saith the LORD of hosts, and I will remove the iniquity of that land in one day (3:9).

This is undoubtedly another reference to the Messiah, who this time is called "the stone" (cf. Isa. 28:16; Ps. 118:22; Matt. 21:42; Acts 4:11; Eph. 2:20-21). To the

Gentile nations He is the stone that will crush their dominion at His second coming (see Dan. 2:34-35, 44-45). To *Israel* He is the stone of stumbling (Rom. 9:31-33). To the *believer* He is the cornerstone of the spiritual building of which each saved one is a part (Eph. 2:19-22).

In Zechariah's vision this stone is said to have "seven eyes." *Eyes* in Scripture speak of intelligence. With the use of the number *seven,* the number of perfection, the figure symbolizes perfect intelligence and wisdom. Christ truly is "the wisdom of God" (I Cor. 1:24). It is also said that the stone has an engraving upon it, but there is no direct statement as to just what this engraving is. Possibly it has to do with the then future incarnation of the Saviour. An ancient writer has said: "It signifies Him who had His birth in virgin-earth, but framed skillfully by the power of the Holy Spirit" (Lapide, quoted by Irenaeus).[16] Undoubtedly the engraving speaks in some way of the preparation of the Messiah, the One "altogether lovely."

The "one day" of this verse refers, as already brought out, to the future day of the Lord, the day of judgment for Israel's foes, and the day of blessing (preceded by judgment) for Israel.

"In that day, saith the LORD of hosts, shall ye call every man his neighbor under the vine and under the fig tree" (3:10). These words indicate the universal peace and prosperity of that future day. A similar expression is used of the reign of Solomon (I Kings 4:25). This prophecy looks forward to that day when "a greater than Solomon" shall reign, a time when righteousness and

[16]Pusey, p. 359.

peace shall pervade the whole earth. May that day soon come!

6. *The Vision of the Candlestick and the Two Olive Trees (4:1-14)*

"And the angel that talked with me came again, and waked me, as a man that is wakened out of his sleep" (4:1). Once more the interpreting angel comes to the prophet, this time to awaken him out of a coma of spiritual exhaustion into which he has fallen as a result of the previous vision seen. It is evident that this is not physical sleep, for he speaks of himself being awakened "*as* a man that is wakened out of his sleep."

> And [the angel] said unto me, What seest thou? And I said, I have looked, and behold a candlestick all of gold, with a bowl upon the top of it, and his seven lamps thereon, and seven pipes to the seven lamps, which are upon the top thereof: and two olive trees by it, one upon the right side of the bowl, and the other upon the left side thereof (4:2-3).

The usual procedure follows. Zechariah is shown another vision and then questioned by the angel as to what he sees. At the angel's interrogation, the prophet tells what he observes in this vision. This time he sees "a candlestick all of gold." At the top of this candlestick is a bowl, a vessel for the oil, which flows from it to the candlestick. On this one candlestick there are seven lamps, with a little pipe running for each of these lamps to the bowl of oil at the top, in order to provide a supply for each. Then beside the candlestick Zechariah sees two "olive trees." One olive tree is on the right side of the candlestick and the other on its left side.

The *candlestick* is the central feature of this vision. It is doubtless similar to and represents the seven-pronged golden candlestick which was in the holy place of the tabernacle (and later of the temple). That candlestick speaks of Christ, who said, "I am the light of the world" (John 8:12; 9:5). It also symbolizes that which Christ's people should be, as He said of His own, "Ye are the light of the world." The candlestick represented what Israel was intended to be—a light shining for God to the rest of the world. The candlestick thus may be said to signify *witnessing*, as do also the two olive trees. The oil is a type of the Holy Spirit, the source of all true testimony for God.

Other features are of interest. The *gold* speaks of divine appointment, and the *sevens* of completion and perfection, since seven is the perfect number both in Scripture and in nature.

Beside the candlestick stand two olive trees, symbolic of fruitful witnessing. From these two olive trees, spouts run to the bowl. The oil empties directly from the olive trees through these spouts into the bowl, from which it circulates into the seven lamps of the candlestick. In the temple worship the oil for the candlestick was provided by the people's gifts and placed in the lamps by the priests. But here in this vision God does the work directly, the oil flowing into the bowl apart from any human agency.

What two persons do these two trees represent? No doubt the prophecy found an immediate fulfillment in

Joshua and Zerubbabel, the high priest and the governor, with their witnessing to Israel in the restored temple.

But the vision must also look beyond this. Probably these are the two witnesses (olive trees) referred to in Revelation 11:3-12 who witness in Jerusalem during the tribulation period yet to come, during the still future seventieth week of Daniel 9. Some Bible students conjecture that these two witnesses are groups,[17] others believe them to be two individuals, possibly Moses and Elijah,[18] or Enoch and Elijah.[19] The most reasonable interpretation is that they are two Spirit-led individuals of the last days who mightily witness for God in the spirit and power of the prophets of old.[20]

> So I answered and spake to the angel that talked with me, saying, What are these, my lord? Then the angel that talked with me answered and said unto me, Knowest thou not what these be? And I said, No, my lord (4:4-5).

The curiosity of the prophet is again aroused and he asks the interpreting angel to explain. The angel then expresses surprise that Zechariah cannot interpret the vision he has just seen.

> Then he answered and spake unto me, saying, This is the word of the LORD unto Zerubbabel, saying, Not by might, nor by power, but by my spirit, saith the LORD of hosts (4:6).

---

[17]See e.g. H. A. Ironside, *Lectures on the Revelation*, p. 192.
[18]Held by Fausset, Bengel, Bede and Dusterdieck. See W. E. Biederwolf, *The Millennium Bible*, p. 613.
[19]"The early church almost universally believed [this]," *ibid.*
[20]See John F. Walwoord, *The Revelation of Jesus Christ*, p. 179.

This is one of the truly great verses of the entire Bible. The word here translated "might" speaks of the strength of many; that rendered "power" refers to the strength of one. "The two might be taken to express human strength and power of every description—physical, mental, and moral—individual, or the combined strength of the multitude. All of themselves can neither advance nor retard the accomplishment of His purpose."[21] Just as the lamps of this candlestick have no power to shine of themselves, so the real power by which the nation Israel (or an individual child of God today) can shine for Him must come from His Holy Spirit. True witnessing is done only through the power of the Holy Spirit as He energizes the witness. "But ye shall receive power, after that the Holy Ghost is come upon you: and ye shall be witnesses unto me" (Acts 1:8).

> Who art thou, O great mountain? Before Zerubbabel thou shalt become a plain: and he shall bring forth the headstone thereof with shoutings, crying, Grace, grace unto it (4:7).

In the power of the Holy Spirit Zerubbabel is to rebuild the temple, and the mountain of difficulty shall become before him a plain. This man who some fifteen years previously had laid the cornerstone of the temple amid great rejoicing (mingled with tears of sorrow) is yet to complete the work. He will "bring forth the headstone thereof with shoutings, crying, Grace, grace unto it." According to custom, the leader or governor of a people would lay the foundation and also the crowning topstone of public buildings. Thus it is prophesied that

[21]Baron, p. 137.

Zerubbabel will bring forth the headstone of the temple and give it to the workmen to place on the top of the completed building.

This is also no doubt another prophecy of the Messiah, who is *the* cornerstone. "Christ is also the *Foundation* and *Top-Stone* (3:9; 4:7). God works *from* Christ and *to* Christ. All the counsels of God center in Him."[22] " 'Shoutings,' of acclamation, 'with a great shout of joy,' accompanied the foundation of the literal Temple (Ezra 3:11, 13). So shoutings of 'Hosanna' greeted the Saviour in entering Jerusalem (Matt. 21:9), when about to *complete* the purchase of salvation by His death: His Body being *the second temple*, or place of God's inhabitation (John 2:20, 21)."[23] With regard to the Lord Jesus, the Messiah, God's grace does indeed rest upon Him who brought grace and truth into the world (John 1:17).

> Moreover the word of the LORD came unto me, saying, The hands of Zerubbabel have laid the foundation of this house; his hands shall also finish it; and thou shalt know that the LORD of hosts hath sent me unto you (4:8-9).

Apparently these words and those that immediately follow come direct from Jehovah to Zechariah without the service of the interpreting angel. The vision just seen is connected with the rebuilding of the temple, and the prophecy is given that it shall be finished by Zerubbabel. There is also another intimation of the Trinity: the prophet is told that he shall know that Jehovah of hosts hath sent "me" (i.e., Jehovah the Word, the second Per-

[22]Max Reich, *The Messianic Hope of Israel*, p. 94.
[23]Jamieson, Fausset and Brown, IV, p. 672.

son of the Trinity) to "you" (i.e., to Zechariah and his people).

> For who hath despised the day of small things?
> For they shall rejoice, and shall see the plummet in
> the hand of Zerubbabel with those seven; they are
> the eyes of the LORD, which run to and fro through
> the whole earth (4:10).

Some of those who recalled the glory of the original temple were skeptical concerning this smaller restoration, and were evidently "despising it" (cf. Ezra 3:12). So the Lord asks the question: "Who hath despised the day of small things?" These beginnings may seem small, but this restoration to the land will eventually result in the birth of the Messiah, with all the blessings attendant to that wondrous event. The latter part of the verse may be rendered: "They, even those seven eyes of the Lord (3:9) which run to and fro through the whole earth, shall rejoice and see [i.e., shall rejoicingly see] the plummet [literally, the stone of tin] in the hand of Zerubbabel."[24] The *plummet*, a line with a weight at the end to determine verticality, speaks of the fact that God is setting out now to complete the work.

"Then answered I, and said unto him, What are these two olive trees upon the right side of the candlestick and upon the left side thereof?" (4:11). Other features of the vision have now been explained to the prophet's satisfaction. But he is still uncertain about the two olive trees. So he asks the question, "What are these?"

"And I answered again, and said unto him, What be these two olive branches which through the two golden

[24]Thomas V. Moore, as cited in *ibid.*

pipes empty the golden oil out of themselves?" (4:12).
Another feature which Zechariah wishes to ask about
concerns the two olive branches (evidently there is a
very fruitful branch on each tree) which are emptying
forth the golden oil (this means golden in color)
through the two golden spouts into the bowl from
whence in turn the oil passes into the candlestick. Evidently the imagery is that of olives coming from the
trees and giving forth their oil into these spouts. This
in turn passes through the pipes to supply the exhaust-
less fuel for the candlestick.

> And he answered me and said, Knowest thou not
> what these be? And I said, No, my lord. Then said
> he, These are the two anointed ones, that stand by
> the Lord of the whole earth (4:13-14).

Zechariah apparently should have had some idea as to
these figures from the portion of the vision previously
explained to him, for he is asked, "Knowest thou not
what these be?" To this question he replies in the negative. He is then told that these represent "the two
anointed ones" (literal Hebrew, "sons of oil") through
whom the supply of oil comes. Joshua and Zerubbabel,
the leaders of the people, represent the priestly and
kingly offices. Both priest and king were anointed with
oil for their offices, representing the enduement of the
Holy Spirit for service. Thus they are "the anointed
ones." They are empowered by the Holy Spirit in order
that they might bring blessing to God's people.

As previously suggested, in immediate fulfillment
these two witnesses are Joshua and Zerubbabel, but there
will yet be a final fulfillment in the two witnesses of

Revelation 11. In the last analysis, the great power of these two witnesses is that they are standing "by the Lord of the whole earth." Do you want to live for God, to witness acceptably for Christ? Then are you living in God's presence? Are you standing by the Lord of the whole earth? Remember, "not by might, nor by power, but by my Spirit, saith the LORD of hosts."

7. *The Vision of the Flying Roll (5:1-4)*

Up to this point the visions have spoken of blessing for Israel. The first four visions foretold outward prosperity for Israel and Jerusalem. The fifth and sixth visions tell of inward blessing as the nation looks "unto him whom they have pierced" (Zech. 12:10) and God "removes the iniquity of that land in one day" (Zech. 3:9).

The seventh and eighth visions present a darker picture. These two visions—the flying roll, and the woman in the ephah—tell of the judgment that must precede the blessing. "For the time is come that judgment must begin at the house of God: and if it first begin at us, what shall be the end of them that obey not the gospel of God?" (I Peter 4:17).

God has two ways of dealing with sin and wickedness. The first is that of *grace.* If sinners turn in repentance and faith to Him, He delights to forgive and cleanse sin on the basis of the death of His Son—His righteous Servant, the Branch—"who bore our sin in his own body on the tree" (I Peter 2:24). But if sinners persist in their wickedness and refuse to receive God's grace, then His method of dealing with sin is that of *judgment.*

> Sin must be purged away, iniquity must be
> stamped out in the city of God; and when the sin-
> ner is so wedded to his sin that he is no longer
> separable from it, he becomes the object of God's
> curse, and must be cleansed away from the earth.[25]

These visions of judgment should bring to mind the
very solemn thought that one must never construe God's
love and grace as giving license to think that sin is a
light, unimportant thing. On the contrary, the price
God had to pay to redeem men from sin should bring
to each mind in a very forcible way "the exceeding sin-
fulness of sin." (Rom. 7:13).

These visions of chapter 5 show the time of darkness
and of degradation that must take place before the opening visions of blessing for Israel will finally be fulfilled.

> Then I turned, and lifted up mine eyes, and
> looked, and behold a flying roll. And he said unto
> me, What seest thou? And I answered, I see a flying
> roll; the length thereof is twenty cubits, and the
> breadth thereof ten cubits (5:1-2).

The prophet turns and is this time shown a flying roll.
He describes this flying roll which he sees. It is a wide,
unrolled scroll which is in motion. It must certainly be
open, or he could not see and determine the dimen-
sions so accurately. It is of great size: 20 by 10 cubits,
which would be about 30 by 15 feet. It is striking to
notice that this size is the same as that of the holy place
in the tabernacle.[26] (It will be remembered that the

[25]Baron, p. 144.
[26]"The length of the tabernacle is fixed by the five curtains which
were to be on each side, *the breadth of each curtain four cubits* (Ex.
26:1, 2). The whole, including the holy of holies, is determined by

golden candlestick in the previous vision was likewise a
symbol taken from the tabernacle.)   Surely this is no
mere coincidence.   What then does it indicate?   "Men
are not to be judged as to sin by their own measures, or
weighed in their own false balances—*the measure of the
sanctuary* is that by which man's actions are to be
weighed (I Sam. 2:3) ."[27]

> Then said he unto me, This is the curse that
> goeth forth over the face of the whole earth: for
> everyone that stealeth shall be cut off as on this
> side according to it; and everyone that sweareth
> shall be cut off as on that side according to it (5:3) .

The interpreting angel, who has again been speaking
with Zechariah, now tells him just what this scroll represents.   It is "the curse that goeth forth over the face of
the whole earth."   The English word *earth* as here used
is not quite accurate, as the expression refers not to the
whole *earth* but rather to the *whole land* of Israel.   Israel
alone was placed under the Mosaic law and shall be
judged by it.   It is never said that any other nation was
ever placed under the law.[28]

the *twenty boards* on each side, *a cubit and a half, the breadth of each
board* (Ex. 26:16, 18).   The breadth is fixed by the *six boards*, i.e.
nine cubits, with the *two boards for the corners of the tabernacle in
the two sides* (Ex. 26:22, 23).   Josephus gives the whole 30 cubits
long (the holy of holies being 10 cubits square) 10 broad (Ant. 3.
6.3)."   Pusey, p. 365.

[27]C. H. H. Wright, as cited in Baron, pp. 147-8.

[28]See Rom. 3:19.   However, this does not mean that the Gentile
world was (and is) without responsibility.   Romans 2 makes it clear
that "the Gentiles, which have not the law (i.e. Mosaic), . . . show
the work of the law written in their hearts, their conscience also bearing witness" and they are thus "a law unto themselves" (verses 14-15).
Therefore "as many as have sinned without law should also perish
without law.   And as many as have sinned in the law shall be judged
by the law" (verse 12).

It is specified in this verse that the scroll is written "on this side" and "on that side," or in other words on both front and back. Two of the commandments are especially mentioned: that against stealing (eighth commandment) and that against swearing falsely in the name of Jehovah (third commandment). These are the middle commandments of the second and first tables of the law respectively, and so no doubt represent the entire law. The two sides of the roll probably represent the two tables of the law, the first having to do with man's relationship to God, the second with his relationship to his fellow men.

> I will bring it forth, saith the LORD of hosts, and it shall enter into the house of the thief, and into the house of him that sweareth falsely by my name: and it shall remain in the midst of his house, and shall consume it with the timber thereof and the stones thereof (5:4).

This is indeed a solemn statement. God says, "I will cause it to go forth" (ASV). Cause what? Why, the curse, the doom, that is to befall the transgressor of God's holy law (Gal. 3:10). For every unrepentant transgressor there is coming a day of judgment at the hand of a holy God. God says of this curse: "I will bring it forth . . . and it shall enter into the house." A man may hide his sin from other men, but not from God. "Be sure your sin will find you out." God's avenging justice will overtake the transgressor even in the place he thinks he is the safest—in his own house. The statement "and it shall abide in the midst of the house" (ASV) speaks of the permanence of God's judgment on the wicked. The

word here translated *abide (remain* in *AV)* has the
thought in it of "to spend the night." God's curse rests
on the transgressor both by day and by night. The chastisement which often overtakes transgressors in this life
is but a foretoken of the terrible day of God's wrath
which shall yet come (see Jude 14-15).

But the climax has not been reached even yet. The
transgressor brings a curse not only upon himself, but
upon his very possessions—his house shall consume
away. In its broad outline this vision refers to judgment
which must come upon Israel before final millennial
blessing. At the same time, however, there is a very real
application to be made to any transgressor of God's holy
law, be he Jew or Gentile. If you are a transgressor, a
sinner—and the Bible affirms that you are, for "all have
sinned and come short of the glory of God" (Rom. 3:23)
—there is but one way in which you can escape the curse
of God, and that is by having your sins cleansed through
the blood of Jesus Christ, God's Son, who came to this
earth and "made purification of sins" (Heb. 1:3, ASV).
Receive Him now as your Saviour.

8. *The Vision of the Woman in the Ephah* (5:5-11)

This is the second of the visions of judgment found in
Zechariah 5. The two "together set forth the full and
final removal, not only of the *guilt* of sin, but of sin itself
(especially in its final and yet future form of *'wickedness'*
or *lawlessness*) —and that by means of judgment—from
off the 'Holy Land,' and from the very presence of His
redeemed and purified people."[29]

29Baron, p. 155.

> Then the angel that talked with me went forth,
> and said unto me, Lift up now thine eyes, and see
> what is this that goeth forth. And I said, What is
> it? And he said, This is an ephah that goeth forth.
> He said moreover, This is their resemblance
> through all the earth (5:5-6).

As in 2:3 the angel now goes forth, probably to meet
another angel. He then calls Zechariah's attention to a
new vision being shown him.

Zechariah once more asks: "What is it?" The description that follows is again a picture of wickedness and
judgment. This time the *wickedness* is traced to its
origin, and *judgment* is pronounced upon that place of
origin. The prophet sees "an ephah." This is a measure
holding just a little more than our bushel. It signifies
something having come to the full and being ready for
judgment: in other words, God has measured Israel's sin
and will bring·it to judgment.

The prophet is further told that "this is their resem-
blance through all the earth" (or literally, "through all
the land"). The meaning is that this is the aspect of
things throughout the whole land.

> And, behold, there was lifted up a talent of lead:
> and this is a woman that sitteth in the midst of the
> ephah. And he said, This is wickedness. And he
> cast it into the midst of the ephah; and he cast
> the weight of lead upon the mouth thereof (5:7-8).

While the prophet watches, he sees the lid of the "bushel
basket" (which consists of a large piece of lead) lifted
up. Then when the lid is removed, he observes that in-
side the basket is a woman (literally, "one woman"). A

woman, as used symbolically in Scripture, usually speaks of religious evil (see for examples Matt. 13:33; I Tim. 2:12; Rev. 2:20; 17:1-7). What does this woman whom Zechariah sees represent? The interpretation is given by the angel in the words "This is wickedness," which explains that the woman represents evil.

As Zechariah continues to watch, the woman apparently attempts to escape but is cast down, and the lid of lead is replaced upon the basket. Thus the woman—that is, wickedness—is sealed by this large weight within the ephah.

> Then lifted I up mine eyes, and looked, and, behold, there came out two women, and the wind was in their wings; for they had wings like the wings of a stork: and they lifted up the ephah between the earth and the heaven (5:9).

Now as Zechariah observes, something further takes place—the basket is lifted up "between the earth and the heaven." This is done by two women who have wings like the wings of a stork, an unclean bird (Lev. 11:19). They also speak in a symbolic way of evil and their sole function is to carry the measure to Babylon (or *Shinar*).

"Then said I to the angel that talked with me, Whither do these bear the ephah? And he said unto me, To build it an house in the land of Shinar: and it shall be established, and set there upon her own base" (5:10-11). The prophet now seeks information concerning the destination of these women bearing the ephah basket, as he asks the interpreting angel: "Whither do these bear the ephah?" The origin of Israel's great sin of past times— *idolatry*—is now traced to Babylon, the place where all

idolatry started. Of this wickedness in the basket it is
stated that "it shall be set there upon her own base." It
is returned to Babylon, and thus Babylon is marked for
judgment. For this reason the Jews are told to leave it
(Zech. 2:7). The term *Shinar* (see Gen. 11:2) refers to
"Babylonia in its fullest extent."[30]

Again there is both a local fulfillment in the near
destruction to come upon Babylon, and a final and distant fulfillment in the judgment of *spiritual Babylon,*
"the confusion into which the whole social order of the
world has fallen under Gentile world-dominion,"[31] in
the last days as so vividly pictured in Revelation 17—18.
"For more than 2000 years, ever since the Babylonian
exile, the Jews have been free from idolatry; but the full
accomplishment of the prophecy is yet future, when all
sins shall be purged from Israel on their return to Palestine and conversion to Christ."[32]

9. *The Vision of the Four Chariots* (6:1-8)

Chapter 6 of Zechariah's prophecy contains the last
two visions granted to the prophet: *the four chariots*
(6:1-8) and *the crowning of Joshua* (6:9-15). The first
of these—the vision of the four chariots—is interpreted
in verses 5 and 6. It speaks of judgment upon the great
world power, with again a near and a far application
from point of time of fulfillment.

"And I turned, and lifted up mine eyes, and looked,
and, behold, there came four chariots out from between
two mountains; and the mountains were mountains of

[30]Robert Young, *Analytical Concordance to the Bible,* p. 880.
[31]Scofield, p. 724.
[32]Jamieson, Fausset and Brown, IV, p. 675.

brass" (6:1). As Zechariah looks he sees a vision con-
sisting of four chariots coming out from between two
brass mountains. These four chariots are war chariots,
and thus signify *judgment*. The two mountains are said
to be of brass. Some Bible students consider these to be
actual mountains such as Mount Moriah and the Mount
of Olives.[33] It is certain that they refer in a symbolic
sense to *strength* (the Bible uses both *mountains* and
brass in this way), and to *judgment* (brass often symbolizes judgment in Scripture).

"In the first chariot were red horses; and in the second
chariot black horses; and in the third chariot white
horses; and in the fourth chariot grizzled and bay horses"
(6:2-3). The four chariots are described in terms of the
horses that draw them. The first has *red* horses pulling
it, the second *black*, the third *white*, and the fourth
grizzled and *bay* horses. In the usual Scripture sym-
bolism *red* speaks of *war*, *black* of *famine* and *death*,
white of *victory*, and *grizzled* of *pestilence* (cf. Ezek.
14:21; Rev. 6:1-8). The drivers of these chariots are not
mentioned at this time.

> Then I answered and said unto the angel that
> talked with me, What are these, my lord? And the
> angel answered and said unto me, These are the
> four spirits of the heavens, which go forth from
> standing before the Lord of all the earth (6:4-5).

Naturally Zechariah is puzzled and once more seeks an
explanation for the vision given him. The interpretation is then given. This interpretation indicates plainly
that the chariots do not represent the four world em-

[33]See Biederwolf, p. 289.

pires of Daniel 2 and 7 (as held by some writers) [34] but are rather four spirits, or angels. They may well be linked with the four angels of Revelation 7:1-3.

"The black horses which are therein go forth into the north country; and the white go forth after them; and the grizzled go forth toward the south country" (6:6). The destinations of the first three chariots are thus specified. The black horses are being sent unto the north country, and the white go after them. The grizzled are sent to the south country. So far as a near fulfillment of this prophecy is concerned, the north country refers to Babylon, and the south country to Egypt. In the far fulfillment—the final and complete fulfillment spoken of in the book of Revelation—these terms refer to the great northern and southern powers of the last days.

> And the bay went forth, and sought to go that they might walk to and fro through the earth: and he said, Get you hence, walk to and fro through the earth. So they walked to and fro through the earth (6:7).

Only the *red* horses remain unaccounted for, and the term *bay* (or literally, "strong") apparently refers to these horses. These last are instructed: "Get you hence, walk to and fro through the earth." So it is evident that they are not sent to any specific section as were the others.

"Then cried he upon me, and spake unto me, saying, Behold, these that go toward the north country have quieted my spirit in the north country" (6:8). To conclude this particular vision, the interpreting angel speaks

[34]*Ibid.*

concerning those horses that went to the north country. The message from the Lord Jehovah is that they "have quieted my spirit in the north country." This means that the judgment executed there has satisfied the justice of Jehovah.

The close connection between this vision and the first one given Zechariah (1:7-17) should be carefully observed. At the beginning of this unforgettable night the prophet saw angel riders, led by the preincarnate Christ, appearing to give their reports to Jehovah after riding "to and fro through the earth." Their report that the wicked nations were at rest while God's people were sorely distressed greatly displeased the Lord.

Now in the present vision, shown to Zechariah just before the break of dawn, the angels are seen going forth, not to reconnoiter as before, but to execute God's judgment upon the nations. This judgment falls on them especially because of their treatment of His ancient people, whom God has not cast away in spite of their failures. "I say then, Hath God cast away his people? God forbid" (Rom. 11:1).

This vision then "sets forth God's control of all destructive agencies used by him in the punishment of the nations deserving His wrath."[35] For the detailed picture of these judgments as they will yet take place on this earth, the reader should study carefully Revelation 6-18, noting there the seal, the trumpet, and the vial judgments.

10. *The Crowning of Joshua* (6:9-15)

Before this last of the ten visions is considered, the

[35]H. A. Ironside, *Notes on the Minor Prophets*, p. 360.

earlier nine should be reviewed. These were:

a. *The horses and the man among the myrtles* (1:7-17). Judgment upon the nations that had persecuted Israel and rich blessing for them in their land yet to be their experience with God "comforting Jerusalem."

b. *The four horns* (1:18-19). The four great world powers that would be instrumental in scattering Israel.

c. *The four workmen* (1:20-21). God's agents that bring judgment upon these nations that have scattered Israel.

d. *The man with the measuring line* (2:1-13). Jerusalem's future deliverance and restoration.

e. *The clothing of Joshua, the high priest* (3:1-10). Israel's future cleansing when they "look unto him whom they have pierced."

f. *The candlestick and the two olive trees* (4:1-14). Israel's witness during the period of the great tribulation.

g. *The flying roll* (5:1-4). The judgment of the wicked among Israel, which must precede the millennial blessing.

h. *The woman in the ephah* (5:5-11). Wickedness of Israel traced to its source in Babylon and the judgment of (spiritual) Babylon foretold (cf. Rev. 17-18).

i. *The four war chariots* (6:1-8). God's judgment upon the nations finally executed.

Now as a climax and culmination of all the visions, the prophet symbolically crowns Joshua, the high priest. Joshua here is a type of Christ, our great High Priest (Heb. 4:14). This vision speaks of the second coming of Christ, at which time He who is already our Priest shall

be crowned "King of kings, and Lord of lords" (Rev.
19:16). Receiving then "the throne of his father David,"
He will "reign over the house of Jacob forever; and of
his kingdom there shall be no end" (Luke 1:32-33).

> And the word of the Lord came unto me, saying,
> Take of them of the captivity, even of Heldai, of
> Tobijah, and of Jedaiah, which are come from
> Babylon, and come thou the same day, and go into
> the house of Josiah the son of Zephaniah; then take
> silver and gold, and make crowns, and set them
> upon the head of Joshua the son of Josedech, the
> high priest (6:9-11).

There is considerable disagreement among the Bible
commentators as to whether this concluding portion of
the first section of the book is an additional vision or an
actual occurrence. It seems best to consider it as another
vision since the formula by which it is introduced ("and
the word of the Lord came unto me") is the same as that
used previously in 1:7 and 4:8 to introduce visions. The
picture, as already brought out, is that of Joshua being
crowned as a type of Christ, the Branch, who is both
King and Priest.

The men mentioned as coming from Babylon are apparently representatives of those Israelites still in captivity, and they are called simply as witnesses of the
scene. Nothing further concerning them is known. They
had come from Babylon to bring an offering for the
temple, which was then being built. They doubtless
represent those from "far off" (6:15) who shall come to
worship the great King of kings when He reigns in
Jerusalem.

Zechariah is told to take silver and gold crowns and with them to crown Joshua. The word *crowns* is in the plural, and suggests a composite crown or a number of diadems (see Rev. 19:12). The meaning of this ceremony is explained in the verses that follow.

> And speak unto him, saying, Thus speaketh the LORD of hosts, saying, Behold the man whose name is The BRANCH; and he shall grow up out of his place, and he shall build the temple of the LORD (6:12).

Once more the symbol of the Branch (cf. 3:8) is used. This speaks prophetically of the Messiah, the Lord Jesus Christ. This passage contains one of the greatest of all the Old Testament Messianic prophecies. Information is now given as to the *person,* the *position,* and the *mission* of the Messiah.

As to the *person* of the Messiah, it is said: "Behold the man whose name is The BRANCH; and he shall grow up out of his place." "Behold the man"—this is reminiscent of the words of Pilate (John 19:5) as he presented Jesus Christ to the people just before He was led out to His death. In Zechariah 6:12, however, attention is not called to the Christ in His suffering and death at His first coming, but to His glorious return as He comes back to this earth to rule and to reign. Here indeed "we see Jesus, who was made a little lower than the angels for the suffering of death, crowned with glory and honor" (Heb. 2:9).

The Messiah is spoken of again as the Branch, and it is said that "he shall grow up out of his place." This suggests His humanity. He is to arise, according to promise, from the seed of Abraham and of David, in the land of Israel. "Out of the dead and barren condition of Judaism, springs this fruitful Branch."[36]

"Even he shall build the temple of the LORD, and he shall bear the glory, and shall sit and rule upon his throne; and he shall be a priest upon his throne: and the counsel of peace shall be between them both" (6:13). Now the Messiah's *position* is described in terms of His *offices*. The statement that "he shall be a priest upon his throne" definitely proves that the prophecy looks far beyond Joshua personally to Jesus, which name by the way is the Greek form of the Hebrew *Joshua*. The Joshua of Zechariah's day could never have been a king because he was not from the kingly line of David but rather from the priestly line of Aaron. Neither could Zerubbabel, who was from David's kingly line, ever have been a priest, for that office could only be held in Old Testament times by those who were from the tribe of Levi. But of the Messiah it is said definitely that He will be a great King, the descendant of David, and also that He will be a Priest: "The LORD hath sworn, and will not repent, Thou art a priest forever after the order of Melchizedek" (Ps. 110:4). The priestly ministry of the Lord Jesus Christ is beautifully and fully described in the New Testament epistle to the Hebrews. As Priest, He offered a sacrifice for sin, and that sacrifice was Himself. As our everliving High Priest, He now intercedes for His own before the throne of God (Heb. 7:25).

Not only is the Messiah to be a Priest, according to

[36]Max Reich, p. 94.

this great prophecy, but also a King. In the type, or picture prophecy, Joshua was already a priest, but to this dignity were added the crowns that spoke of kingship. So the Lord Jesus is even now a Priest serving in the true holy of holies in heaven and seated upon His Father's throne (Rev. 3:21). Someday He is coming again to the earth to take up His great power and reign forever upon the throne of His earthly father David. That time has not yet come, but it is certain and sure (Heb. 9:28).

As to the *mission* of the Messiah it is said twice over that He shall "build the temple of the LORD." Once again it can be seen that the prophecy looks beyond Joshua the high priest, for he did not build the then present temple—Zerubbabel did that—and on to the Messiah King who will some day build the glorious millennial temple, described so fully in Ezekiel 40-48.

At the same time however there is undoubtedly a deeper significance to this statement, for we are told in the New Testament that Christ is building a temple even now—a temple composed of living stones—of each one who receives Him as Saviour and through faith in Him is born again (see, e.g., Eph. 2:21; I Peter 2:5).

Finally, the prophecy indicates that "he shall bear thee glory." In the day when this living temple is completed, and when He reigns supreme on this earth, the glory shall be His alone. For a picture of this majestic reign, read Psalm 72:6-19. Is this great Messiah, this wonderful Saviour, being glorified in your life now?

Verse 13 closes with the words "and the counsel of peace shall be between them both." To whom does this "both" refer? "Not [between] the Branch and Jehovah, nor the Branch and an ideal priest . . . but the king and the priest who sit upon the throne united in one person, the Branch."[37]

"And the crowns shall be to Helem, and to Tobijah, and to Jedaiah, and to Hen the son of Zephaniah, for a memorial in the temple of the LORD" (6:14). The crowns were not to belong to Joshua personally but were to be in the charge of these deputies, the same ones previously mentioned in verse 10. *Helem* here stands for Heldiah as used there, and *Hen* is no doubt another name for Josiah.

> And they that are far off shall come and build
> in the temple of the Lord, and ye shall know that
> the LORD of hosts hath sent me unto you. And this
> shall come to pass, if ye will diligently obey the
> voice of the LORD your God (6:15).

The reference to those "that are far off" is an allusion to the Gentile nations that shall be blessed in that day of Messiah's glory. It is said that they will "build in the temple of Jehovah" which speaks of their participation in these great events. But for both Israelites and Gentiles alike participation in these things depends on faith and obedience: "And this shall come to pass, if ye will diligently obey the voice of the LORD your God." With these words, section one of the book concludes. The reader is now ready for the great second division of Zechariah.

[37]Talbot W. Chambers, "Zechariah," The Minor Prophets, Lange's Commentary, p. 53.

2

THE QUESTION OF BETHEL AND THE ANSWER OF THE LORD
(7:1—8:23)

FROM VISIONS, the style of the book now changes to direct discourse from the Lord through Zechariah. The rest of the book is largely an amplification of that which has gone before, with a number of very striking parallels.

THE QUESTION OF BETHEL (7:1-3)

And it came to pass in the fourth year of king Darius, that the word of the LORD came unto Zechariah in the fourth day of the ninth month, even in Chisleu; when they had sent unto the house of God Sherezer and Regemmelech, and their men, to pray before the LORD, and to speak unto the priests which were in the house of the LORD of hosts, and to the prophets, saying, Should I weep in the fifth month, separating myself, as I have done these so many years? (7:1-3).

By comparison with Zechariah 1:1, 7 it will be seen that about two years have now elapsed since the occurrence of the visions described in chapters 1—6. This central section of the book revolves around a question asked concerning a fast in the fifth month. The deputation asking this question comes some time in advance of this date (to be exact, in the ninth month of the preceding year) to get this information in ample time.

"The house of God" is mentioned in our Authorized Version (7:2). The original word is *Bethel,* which means "house of God." Evidently here, however, the reference is not to the temple, but to the widely known city of that name—Bethel itself. The meaning of the statement is simply this: the people of the city of Bethel sent a deputation composed of the men mentioned by name, and others not named, to ask the question about the fast. This forms the background of the prophecy which follows.

The delegation speaks unto those considered authorities in the things of God—the *priests* and the *prophets.* Their question concerns the propriety of a certain fast then being observed. Now only one fast—the Day of Atonement—was required of Israel by God[1] but a number of additional fasts had been added by the people themselves. This fast of the fifth month was in remembrance of the destruction of Jerusalem and its temple by the Babylonians (II Kings 25:8; Jer. 52:12). This fast is said to be observed even down to the present day by some pious Jewish people.

[1]This seems to be the general understanding of commentators. "The only fast day enjoined by the Law of Moses was the great Day of Atonement on the tenth day of the seventh month" W. J. Deane, "The Book of Zechariah," *Pulpit Commentary,* XIV, 67. However, it should be added that even the command concerning this occasion (Lev. 23:27) does not directly specify fasting but orders that "ye shall afflict your souls," an injunction that has been interpreted by Jewish authorities as involving fasting.

Now that the temple and Jerusalem are again prospering, the people begin to wonder if there is any further need for such a fast, and thus the question is asked.

THE REPLY OF JEHOVAH (7:4-14)

Then came the word of the LORD of hosts unto me, saying, Speak unto all the people of the land, and to the priests, saying, When ye fasted and mourned in the fifth and seventh month, even those seventy years, did ye at all fast unto me, even to me? (7:4-5).

The Lord Jehovah now gives His answer to the question through His prophet Zechariah. Evidently the question had been puzzling others in Judah and all needed this message from the Lord, so the answer comes not just to this small delegation but to all Israel. A second fast in the seventh month, mentioned in addition to that in the fifth month, commemorated the murder of Gedaliah, the governor Nebuchadnezzar installed after the fall of Jerusalem, who was murdered by Ishmael (Jer. 41:43).

God, in His answer, indicates that these fasts, not specifically commanded by Him, had been carried out as a mere formality, not as an act of true repentance. Of course they regretted the destruction of their country, but there was no real sorrow for their sin which had caused this judgment to fall.

"And when ye did eat, and when ye did drink, did not ye eat for yourselves, and drink for yourselves?" (7:6). God says that their fasting, like their feasting, was done for themselves and not unto Him, so that one had no more effect so far as He was concerned than the other.

Do not think that because you go through various formalities of religion that all is necessarily well between
you and God. Outward formalities are worthless if the
heart is not right toward God.

> Should ye not hear the words which the LORD
> hath cried by the former prophets, when Jerusalem
> was inhabited and in prosperity, and the cities
> thereof round about her, when men inhabited the
> south and the plain? (7:7).

With these words, God shows that the question of the
people is entirely superfluous since the fact itself is a
matter of indifference. One should indeed be sure that
the religious ceremonies he follows are truly instituted
by God, otherwise they are of very little value at best.
However, the people are reminded that it is of far greater
importance to listen to God's messengers and heed them
than to celebrate a formal fast. "The pure formality of
fasting is of no importance in comparison with hearing
and doing the Word of God."[2]

An amplification of this subject now follows, the definite answer being given finally in 8:19. The cause of
the previous punishment is now cited and then promise
is made of future blessing.

> And the word of the LORD came unto Zechariah,
> saying, Thus speaketh the LORD of hosts, saying,
> Execute true judgment, and show mercy and com-
> passions every man to his brother: and oppress not
> the widow, nor the fatherless, the stranger, nor the
> poor; and let none of you imagine evil against his
> brother in your heart (7:8-10).

[2]C. Fred Lincoln, unpublished notes on Zechariah.

These words contain the picture of what Jehovah had
desired for His people. He desired "true judgment" on
their part, that is, "judgment agreeing with the truth in
all things without any respect of persons or partiality."[3]
The *widow*, the *orphan*, the *stranger*, and the *poor* are
particularly mentioned as being always the special ob-
jects of God's care. Such injunctions as these were often
repeated in the Mosaic law but had been little observed.
The description of the way God's people should walk in
relation to one another is beautiful indeed: "Let none
of you imagine evil against his brother in your heart."

"But they refused to hearken, and pulled away the
shoulder, and stopped their ears, that they should not
hear" (7:11). What Jehovah desired has already been
shown. What the people actually did is now stated.
"They refused to hearken"—the *they* refers of course to
the fathers (or ancestors) of the people to whom Zechariah is now speaking. Of these the prophet says that
they "pulled away the shoulder," which means that they
turned a rebellious shoulder. The picture is that of an
ox or a heifer refusing to let the yoke be placed (for a
similar picture see Neh. 9:29; Hosea 4:16). They also
"stopped their ears, that they should not hear." They
closed their ears to what God spoke to them. "It is
one of the terrible moral consequences of men turning
away from *doing* the will of God, that the more they
hear, the duller their perceptions become, so that in the
end, though having eyes, they see not."[4] God grant that
such may never have to be said of anyone who reads these
lines. The way of blessing is to be not only a *hearer* of

[3]C. H. H. Wright, *Zechariah and His Prophecies*, p. 174.
[4]David Baron, *Visions and Prophecies of Zechariah*, p. 221.

God's Word, but also a *doer* (James 1:22-25). This picture from the history of ancient Israel should be a warning to modern men.

> Yea, they made their hearts as an adamant stone, lest they should hear the law, and the words which the LORD of hosts hath sent in his spirit by the former prophets: therefore came a great wrath from the LORD of hosts (7:12).

The climax is reached with this statement that these disobedient people "made their hearts as an adamant stone." The *adamant* (or diamond) is used here as referring to the hardest of stones, a picture of the hardness of the hearts which refused to listen to God's voice. How awful to think of men hardening their hearts against God Himself! God loves you (see John 3:16) —open your heart to Him and He will bless you.

This verse is especially interesting because it distinguishes two of the great divisions of the Old Testament— the *law* and the *prophets*. The claim of verbal inspiration is clearly and distinctly made when it is stated that these are "the words which Jehovah of hosts had sent by his Spirit" (ASV).

In this seventh chapter of Zechariah's prophecy, verses 8-10 show what Jehovah desired. Verses 11-12 tell what the people actually did. Verses 13-14 indicate what Jehovah had to do.

> Therefore it is come to pass, that as he cried, and they would not hear; so they cried, and I would not hear, saith the LORD of hosts; but I scattered them with a whirlwind among all the nations whom they knew not. Thus the land was desolate after them,

that no man passed through nor returned: for they
laid the pleasant land desolate" (7:13-14) .

Just as the Lord Jehovah had called and they would not
listen, so when the hour of judgment—of retribution—
came to them, then "they cried, and I would not hear,
saith the LORD of hosts." The picture provided of the
complete fulfillment of the previous prophecies of judgment is terrible indeed. For seventy years the land was
desolate. Thus was fulfilled Jehovah's threat to an un-
heeding people. God's Word never fails. Jesus Christ
said: "Heaven and earth shall pass away, but my words
shall not pass away" (Matt. 24:35) .

The chapter closes with the words "for they laid the
pleasant land desolate." The pronoun *they* refers of
course to the Babylonians who were used as instruments
in God's hand to punish His people. The "pleasant
land" is Palestine, the promised land, the land of God's
own choosing.

FUTURE BLESSING FOR ISRAEL (8:1-17)

"Again the word of the LORD of hosts came to me, saying, Thus saith the LORD of hosts; I was jealous for Zion
with great jealousy, and I was jealous for her with great
fury" (8:1-2) . Additional word comes from Jehovah in
this same connection with regard to blessing now that
His wrath is past. There now follows a further statement
as to the blessing yet to come when the Lord comforts
Zion, as foretold in Zechariah's first prophetic vision in
chapter 1. Again God speaks of being jealous for Zion,
and of being angry with her oppressors who have gone

beyond the necessary punishment that He had in mind
for Israel.

> Thus saith the LORD; I am returned unto Zion,
> and will dwell in the midst of Jerusalem: and
> Jerusalem shall be called a city of truth; and the
> mountain of the LORD of hosts the holy mountain
> (8:3).

The blessed truth is announced that God will dwell
again in Jerusalem. Once more it must be said that,
although there was no doubt a very partial fulfillment
in the blessings given Zechariah and his generation, in a
complete and final sense the prophecy remains to be fulfilled in the future in the wonderful millennial kingdom
that will eventually come to Israel. In that day, "Jerusalem shall be called a city of truth." Truth shall be
characteristic of Jerusalem as a city, in sharp contrast to
past conditions there. In former days it has been called
"unclean" (Lam. 1:8-17), "harlot" and "murderer" (Isa.
1:21), "Sodom" and "Egypt" (Rev. 11:8). In the future
"the mountain of the LORD of hosts" (very likely a reference to Mount Moriah, the site of the temple) will
be called "the holy mountain"—holy because set apart
for the true service of God.

There now follows a beautiful picture of the blessedness of Jerusalem in that day when the Lord indeed
dwells in the midst of it.

> Thus saith the LORD of hosts; There shall yet old
> men and old women dwell in the streets of Jeru-
> salem, and every man with his staff in his hand for
> very age. And the streets of the city shall be full

> of boys and girls playing in the streets thereof
> (8:4-5) .

These words reveal the great peace that shall exist in that day. Because of peaceful times, old age shall be common. During war periods, the flower of mankind is destroyed and few live to old age. Not only shall there be many aged people, but the streets will "be full of boys and girls"—another symbol of peace, prosperity, and happiness.

To a people long persecuted and oppressed such blessings seem to be too good to be true, but the Lord asks a question. "Thus saith the LORD of hosts; If it be marvelous in the eyes of the remnant of this people in these days, should it also be marvelous in mine eyes? saith the LORD of hosts" (8:6). Another question asked by the Lord many centuries earlier may be recalled at this point: "Is anything too hard for the Lord?" (Gen. 18:14). He has planned these blessings and He shall bring them to pass.

But this is not all. Still a further promise of blessing is given by Jehovah.

> Thus saith the LORD of hosts; Behold, I will save
> my people from the east country, and from the
> west country; and I will bring them, and they shall
> dwell in the midst of Jerusalem: and they shall be
> my people, and I will be their God, in truth and
> in righteousness (8:7-8) .

How similar this is to a parallel passage in Romans 11:25-27! Proof that this prophecy in Zechariah refers to a still future restoration of Israel is shown by the terms "from the east country" and "from the west country." Those who returned after the Babylonian exile to the Holy Land came only from the *East*. But some day God shall bring His people from both East and West back to their own land. The gracious prophecy is wonderfully clear. How could such a plain prediction have any other than a completely literal fulfillment? All the Old Testament prophetic books are replete with prophecy concerning the blessedness of the millennial kingdom.

> Thus saith the LORD of hosts; Let your hands be strong, ye that hear in these days these words by the mouth of the prophets, which were in the day that the foundation of the house of the LORD of hosts was laid, that the temple might be built (8:9).

With the words "Let your hands be strong," another great passage now opens. This expression is simply an exhortation to be of good courage (see Judges 7:11; II Sam. 16:21). God encourages the people to hear the words spoken "by the mouth of the prophets." The reference is of course to the prophets Haggai and Zechariah, who are speaking to the people the words of Jehovah at this particular time when the temple is being rebuilt. God says that the foundation has been laid in other that the temple might be built. In other words, this time the temple will be finished.

> For before these days there was no hire for man, nor any hire for beast; neither was there any peace to him that went out or came in because of the

affliction: for I set all men every one against his
neighbor (8:10).

God reminds the people that during the time before construction of the temple had been resumed, a time in
which the people were lax and careless in fulfilling their
religious duties to God, they had suffered temporally.
There was unemployment, quarreling, bickering, and
fighting—all because the people were not in the will of
God. They were troubled by enemies without, and in
addition there was internal strife among themselves.

"But now I will not be unto the residue of this people
as in the former days, saith the LORD of hosts" (8:11).
Now that they are obedient to God, in contrast to the
former time of trouble, Jehovah will now go to the op-
posite extreme in blessing Israel.

> For the seed shall be prosperous; the vine shall
> give her fruit, and the ground shall give her in-
> crease, and the heavens shall give their dew; and I
> will cause the remnant of this people to possess all
> these things (8:12).

The thought of this verse seems to be rather difficult to
translate from the Hebrew language into English. Probably the idea is that "the seed of peace, namely the vine,
shall give its fruit, and the ground shall give its increase,
and the heavens shall give their dew." All this is but to
say that the earth and the heavens are to give forth their
blessing for Israel.

> And it shall come to pass, that as ye were a curse
> among the heathen, O house of Judah, and house
> of Israel; so will I save you, and ye shall be a bless-

ing: fear not, but let your hands be strong (8:13).

"This does not mean that they would become a *source* of blessing to the nations, but an *example* of blessedness, and therefore would be employed in a formula of benediction, just as they had been used for an imprecatory formula."[5]

> For thus saith the LORD of hosts; As I thought to punish you, when your fathers provoked me to wrath, saith the LORD of hosts, and I repented not: so again have I thought in these days to do well unto Jerusalem and to the house of Judah: fear ye not (8:14-15).

These words present a striking contrast. God's threats were surely fulfilled, and thus certainly shall His blessings come to pass.

> These are the things that ye shall do; Speak ye every man the truth to his neighbor; execute the judgment of truth and peace in your gates: and let none of you imagine evil in your hearts against his neighbor; and love no false oath: for all these are things that I hate, saith the LORD (8:16-17).

In view of the blessings now promised, here is Jehovah's commandment as to what the people shall do. The two verses present first the positive and then the negative side. On the positive side, they are to administer righteous judgment that will bring about peace. This, God says, is to be done "in your gates." That was the place in which the "courts" of the day were usually held. On the negative side, they are to abstain from evil plots against others and from perjury. The Lord Jehovah

[5]Talbot W. Chambers, "Zechariah," *The Minor Prophets,* Lange's Commentary, XIV, 62.

hates these things as they are contrary to His righteous character.

Fasting Turned to Feasting (8:18-23)

And the word of the Lord of hosts came unto me, saying, Thus saith the Lord of hosts; The fast of the fourth month, and the fast of the fifth, and the fast of the seventh, and the fast of the tenth, shall be to the house of Judah joy and gladness, and cheerful feasts; therefore love the truth and peace (8:18-19).

At last a definite answer is given concerning the fasts previously inquired about (see 7:3). Because of Jehovah's great blessing, they are to be turned to feasting—they shall be "cheerful feasts." As already stated the fast which the Israelites held in the *fifth month* commemorated the destruction of Jerusalem and the temple. That of the *seventh month* was a day of mourning for the murder of the good governor Gedaliah, which crime was committed in connection with the civil strife after the fall of Jerusalem. Now two other fasts are mentioned. That of the *fourth month* commemorated the taking of Jerusalem by the Babylonians and the flight of the seed royal from the city (Jer. 39:2-9; 52:6-7). That of the *tenth month* was a mourning for the beginning of the siege of the city (Jer. 39:1; 52:4). "All these days are still observed as fasts by the Jewish nation in all parts of the earth, for it is still the night of weeping for Israel, and Zion still sits desolate."[6, 7] But thank God for the revelation that this

[6]Baron, p. 249.
[7]The ancient city of Jerusalem, for the first time in literally thousands of years, came under control of Israel in the Six Day War, June 1967.

long, bitter night of weeping for Israel is to be followed inevitably by a wonderful morning of joy and gladness! Sorrow shall be turned into rejoicing. Fasting shall be turned into feasting.

"Therefore," says the prophet, "love the truth and peace." These words emphasize the important fact that divine prophecy should always have a practical effect upon the present life. If today Christians have the assurance that God is going to do wonderful things for them in the future, then they should live for Him right now. This truth is certainly as equally applicable to individual believers in Christ now, as to members of the chosen nation in Zechariah's day. God has revealed that there are great and marvelous things ahead for His children. His children should therefore be doubly determined to live for Him now (I John 3:2-3).

> Thus saith the LORD of hosts; It shall yet come to pass, that there shall come people, and the inhabitants of many cities: and the inhabitants of one city shall go to another, saying, Let us go speedily to pray before the LORD, and to seek the LORD of hosts: I will go also (8:20-21).

In the Hebrew text verse 20 opens with the word *yet*. This emphasizes the significance of the message. Even though it may appear very unlikely in the eyes of Zechariah's generation (or for that matter to people reading these words today) *yet* God is absolutely and assuredly going to do these great things. He reveals that not only individual Israelites, but many people of various nations shall come on pilgrimage to Jerusalem: "There shall come peoples." The word rendered "peoples" means *all* nations.

The inhabitants of one city shall go to those of other cities with the injunction: "Let us go speedily to pray before the LORD [literally, entreat the face of Jehovah], and to seek the LORD of hosts." Surely this must refer to something more than the wonderful spread of the gospel to all nations during the present age, as some commentators would interpret it.[8] This is not a picture of missionaries going to far distant nations with the gospel message, but of people of different nations going to Jerusalem to see Jehovah face to face. Thank God for the assurance that this will be literally fulfilled when the Lord Jesus Christ—the One who said, "He that hath seen me hath seen the Father" (John 14:9) —actually sits and reigns in Jerusalem on the throne of David (Luke 1:32-33). This will take place when He returns to this earth at the second advent. Verse 21 closes with the response of one invited to go to Jerusalem to see the great King. Each one invited replies: "I will go also."

"Yea, many people and strong nations shall come to seek the LORD of hosts in Jerusalem, and to pray before the LORD" (8:22). With these words the thought is completed and the reason definitely given for these nations going to Jerusalem. They go "to seek the LORD of hosts in Jerusalem, and to pray before the LORD." In that great future day, Ezekiel tells us, the name of the city shall be *Jehovah-Shammah*: "the LORD is there" (Ezek. 48:35).

> Thus saith the LORD of hosts; In those days it shall come to pass, that ten men shall take hold

[8]See e.g. E. B. Pusey, *The Minor Prophets*, II, 391.

out of all languages of the nations, even shall take
hold of the skirt of him that is a Jew, saying, We
will go with you: for we have heard that God is
with you (8:23).

A typical example of the attitude of people in that day is
pictured. Ten men of various nations are depicted as
taking hold of the garment of one seen to be a Jew, saying to him: "We will go with you: for we have heard that
God is with you." The definite number ten is used here
simply to indicate an indefinite number of people and to
show how anxious individuals of various nations will be
to join themselves unto the Jew, because the center of
the kingdom is in his land, because the Lord Jehovah
reigns in Zion.

3

THE DOWNFALL OF THE NATIONS AND THE SALVATION OF ISRAEL

(9:1—14:21)

IN THIS THIRD and last great division of Zechariah's prophecy a remarkable picture is given of the judgment of the nations around Israel and of the glorious millennial reign of the Messiah.

THE BURDEN OF HADRACH (9:1-8)

The burden of the word of the LORD in the land of Hadrach, and Damascus shall be the rest thereof: when the eyes of man, as of all the tribes of Israel, shall be toward the LORD (9:1).

The message now to be given is called a *burden*. This word when joined with the name of Jehovah is always used for prophecy and that usually of a threatening nature. The *burden* is a heavy prophecy of judgment. Modern students are not agreed as to exactly what section is referred to in the expression "the land of Hadrach." It is, however, linked with Damascus, which is the center of the prophecy, and therefore must have been in the region of that city. The last part of the verse may best be translated: "for the eye of man and of all the tribes of Israel is toward Jehovah" (ASV). The eyes of all men will be turned upon Jehovah in wonder when these events take place.

> And Hamath also shall border thereby; Tyrus, and Zidon, though it be very wise. And Tyrus did build herself a stronghold, and heaped up silver as the dust, and fine gold as the mire of the streets. Behold, the Lord will cast her out, and he will smite her power in the sea; and she shall be devoured with fire (9:2-4).

Other cities shall share with Damascus the burden of God's wrath. *Hamath* was another chief city of Syria, while *Tyre* and *Sidon* were well-known cities of nearby Phoenicia. Sidon was the older of these two latter cities, Tyre being originally founded as its colony, but the colony soon outstripped the parent city. Tyre is elsewhere spoken of as very wise (Ezek. 28:2-5; cf. I Cor. 1:19, 27), that is, in earthly wisdom. Though it may be very wise and strong, yet it cannot avert the righteous judgment of the Lord. Despite its power, it is to be overthrown. This prophecy was fulfilled some 200 years later, when the city was besieged by Alexander the Great.

> Ashkelon shall see it, and fear; Gaza also shall see it, and be very sorrowful, and Ekron; for her expectation shall be ashamed; and the king shall perish from Gaza, and Ashkelon shall not be inhabited (9:5).

The leading cities of Philistia also are mentioned. They

shall see the destruction that has come on Tyre and Sidon, and they shall be afraid. Three Philistine cities are named in this verse, and a fourth in that just following: Ashkelon, Gaza, Ekron, and Ashdod. Of Gaza it is said that "the king shall perish from Gaza." Earlier conquerors had left the native rulers in nominal charge of their realms, as long as they were submissive. This was not however the policy of Alexander the Great.

> And a bastard shall dwell in Ashdod, and I will cut off the pride of the Philistines. And I will take away his blood out of his mouth, and his abominations from between his teeth: but he that remaineth, even he, shall be for our God, and he shall be as a governor in Judah, and Ekron as a Jebusite (9:6-7).

These verses indicate that strange people of low birth will dwell in Ashkelon, and the nationality of the Philistines will be destroyed. Thus their pride, not affected by other disasters, will be humbled. "The abominations" of Philistia refer to the nation's idolatrous worship. The "blood" is that of the sacrifices made in such worship. This worship is to be cut off. Thank God, however, for the word of grace that eventually a remnant from Philistia is to be saved, and this remnant shall be God's. Even though He righteously must punish evildoers, yet He is always ready to receive those who will turn in sincere repentance and faith to Him.

> And I will encamp about mine house because of the army, because of him that passeth by, and because of him that returneth: and no oppressor shall

pass through them any more: for now have I seen
with mine eyes (9:8) .

Blessed asurance is given that God shall encamp about
"his house" (i.e., His people) for their protection against
their enemies. Never again will there be anyone to op-
press them. Jehovah has looked with favor once more
on His ancient people.

THE COMING KING AND THE DELIVERANCE HE WILL BRING TO ISRAEL (9:9-17)

From predictions of judgment, the prophet now turns
to the subject of the great King who is to come, and to
the peace and deliverance He will bring to Israel. In
this prophecy, as in the rest of Old Testament revelation,
there is no clear distinction drawn between the two
comings of the Messiah. The first and second advents
of Christ are seen in the Old Testament like two great
mountain peaks on the horizon, which from a distance
seem almost to touch each other. When one draws
nearer, however, an extensive valley is found to separate
the two mountains. Thus the long space of time between
the two comings of our Lord was not shown to the
prophets of old.

There are two distinct lines of prophecy in the Old
Testament concerning the coming Messiah. On one
hand, it is prophesied that He will be a Messiah who will
suffer and die. On the other, He is represented as a
Messiah who will rule and reign. These two themes are
summarized by the apostle Peter as "the sufferings of
Christ, and the glory that should follow" (see I Peter
1:10-11) . Peter indicates that the prophets themselves

did not fully understand the distinction between these two types of prophecies, nor the difference in the times of fulfillment. A significant illustration of this is found in Isaiah 61:1-2. Our Lord, when reading this passage in the synagogue at Nazareth, stopped abruptly when He finished those features referring to His first coming, and did not read of those other things to be fulfilled at His second advent (see Luke 4:18-21).

> Rejoice greatly, O daughter of Zion; shout, O daughter of Jerusalem: behold, thy King cometh unto thee: he is just, and having salvation; lowly, and riding upon an ass, and upon a colt the foal of an ass (9:9).

Israel is called on to *rejoice greatly,* to *shout* with joy. Why? Because their King is coming. The prophet does not say *"a* King" but *"thy* King." This King is the promised Messiah who is to redeem Israel. Of Him it is said that "he is just," or *righteous.* The implication is that not only is He Himself personally righteous, but that He is the fountainhead of righteousness. How wonderfully is this fulfilled in Jesus Christ, the only perfect, righteous, and sinless Man who has ever lived on this earth! And He is the One through whom ungodly sinners can be made righteous with the righteousness of God, as they come to Him in faith (Rom. 4:5).

It is further said that this great coming King will "have salvation." The expression does not mean that He has salvation in the same way that a guilty sinner may now have salvation by passing from darkness to light, by being regenerated by the Holy Spirit. It rather means that He *possesses* salvation which He can *bestow* upon others.

Beyond this He is said to be "lowly." Here is the best commentary that can be added to this word:

> Have this mind in you, which also was in Christ Jesus: who, existing in the form of God, counted not the being on an equality with God a thing to be grasped, but emptied himself, taking the form of a servant, being made in the likeness of men; and being found in fashion as a man, he humbled himself, becoming obedient even unto death, yea, the death of the cross (Phil. 2:5-8, ASV).

It should be remembered in this connection that true humility does not consist merely in a person's thinking of himself in low terms, but rather in his not thinking of himself at all. Surely the Lord Jesus Christ was the supreme example of such true humility. He alone of all men thought ever only of the Father's will. He said "not my will but thine be done" to the heavenly Father. He stated that He came "not to be ministered unto but to minister and to give his life a ransom for many."

The verse closes with a picture of the great King, who is so truly humble, "riding upon an ass, and upon a colt the foal of an ass," as He comes to present Himself to Israel at His first advent. This was literally fulfilled in what is usually called the Triumphal Entry of our Lord into Jerusalem on Palm Sunday before His crucifixion. Matthew 21:1-5 makes it clear that this scene was the fulfillment of Zechariah 9:9. How literally these prophecies concerning His first coming were fulfilled! Who dares

to say that the remaining prophecies with regard to His
return shall be any less literally fulfilled!

The verse just studied contains a great prophecy of
the coming King, the Messiah of Israel. It especially
pictures His first advent—"the sufferings of Christ." Beginning with the very next verse, the second coming is in
view, "the glory that should follow." The glorious re-
sults of His return are graphically pictured.

> And I will cut off the chariot from Ephraim, and
> the horse from Jerusalem, and the battle-bow shall
> be cut off: and he shall speak peace unto the
> heathen: and his dominion shall be from sea even
> to sea, and from the river even to the ends of the
> earth (9:10).

The *chariot* spoken of here is the battle chariot, and the
horse is mentioned (as usual in Scripture) as an imple-
ment of warfare. There will be no more need for these
tools of war in that day. Why not? Because this great
King shall "speak peace," not only to Israel, but also to
the nations of the earth who will share in the blessed
peace of the millennium. The fact that His dominion
will be "from sea to sea" is doubtless a general expression
to indicate from any one sea to that which is most distant from it. His rule is also described as being from "the
river to the ends of the earth." *The river* is an expression
used in Scripture to refer to the Euphrates River. "To
the ends of the earth" indicates the universality of this
glorious kingdom.

After showing in a general way the peace that is to
engulf the entire world, the prophecy now deals especially with the blessings to Israel. "As for thee also, by

the blood of thy covenant I have sent forth thy prisoners
out of the pit wherein is no water" (9:11). Why is
Israel to be blessed? Because of their faithfulness to
God? No, but because of the unfailing covenant He has
already made—"by the blood of thy covenant I have sent
forth thy prisoners." Israel in dispersion is spoken of as
being *in prison.* However, the dispersed are to be regathered and restored to their own land. God says:
"Turn you to the stronghold, ye prisoners of hope: even
today do I declare that I will render double unto thee"
(9:12). The people are to return from their dispersion
to the Holy Land. God calls them *prisoners of hope.*
Though dispersed, their case is not hopeless. They are
prisoners who have *hope,* in that they have His promise
concerning their regathering. The Lord says to them,
"I will render double unto thee." By this He means
double *blessing* to make up for the suffering they have
endured.

"When I have bent Judah for me, filled the bow with
Ephraim, and raised up thy sons, O Zion, against thy
sons, O Greece, and made thee as the sword of a mighty
man" (9:13). The method is revealed by which Israel
shall be finally victorious. It is not in anything of their
own strength, but because Jehovah "bends" the battle-
bow, and "fills" it, "stirring up" the sons of Zion against
their enemies. The particular enemy here mentioned is
Greece. Once more it must be said that there was no
doubt a *partial* fulfillment of this prophecy in the victory finally won by the Maccabees against the Greek
ruler of Syria, Antiochus Epiphanes, which took place

in the period of time between the Old and New Testaments.

But a *final* and *complete* fulfillment evidently awaits the last days of this age. "Zion and Greece, as has been well observed by another writer, are in this prophecy of Zechariah opposed to one another as the city of God and the city of the world, and the defeat of Antiochus Epiphanes and his successors at the hands of comparative handfuls of despised Jews, to which this passage may refer primarily, foreshadows the final conflict with world-power, and the judgments to be inflicted on the confederated armies who shall be gathered against Jerusalem, not only directly by the hand of God, but also by the hand of Israel, who shall then be made strong in Jehovah, so that 'the feeble among them shall be as David, and the house of David shall be as God, as the angel of Jehovah before them.'"[1]

"And the LORD shall be seen over them, and his arrow shall go forth as the lightning: and the Lord GOD shall blow the trumpet, and shall go with whirlwinds of the south" (9:14). This battle of Israel against their enemies is described poetically in terms of a thunderstorm, as Jehovah directs His people.

> The LORD of hosts shall defend them; and they shall devour, and subdue with sling stones; and they shall drink, and make a noise as through wine; and they shall be filled like bowls, and as the corners of the altar (9:15).

Not only does Jehovah empower His people for *offense,* but He is also their *defense,* their shield. They are

[1]David Baron, *Visions and Prophecies of Zechariah,* p. 327.

spoken of as "devouring and subduing" their enemies,
not "*with* sling stones," but literally the expression is
simply "the sling stones." This means that they shall
consume their enemies and "their enemies shall fall
under them, as harmless and as of little account as the
sling stones which have missed their aim, and lie as the
road to be passed over."[2] So great is their victory that
they will be "filled" with the blood of their enemies, as
were the *bowls* in which the priests caught the blood of
the sacrifices, which blood would drip from *the corners
of the altar* after the sacrifices were made.

"And the LORD their God shall save them in that day
as the flock of his people: for they shall be as the stones
of a crown, lifted up as an ensign upon his land" (9:16).
In that day when their enemies shall converge upon
them, "the LORD their God shall save them." Spiritual
as well as physical salvation shall come to God's people,
who are here pictured in a familiar way as *sheep*—"the
flock of his people." Then they shall be "as the stones
of a crown, lifted up as an ensign upon his land." While
their enemies are to be trampled under foot as sling
stones, God's people are precious stones like the stones
in a crown. This crown is to be lifted up in the land—
the Holy Land—for all to see.

"For how great is his goodness, and how great is his
beauty! Corn shall make the young men cheerful, and
new wine the maids" (9:17). As the prophet meditates
on this wonderful deliverance and blessing for Israel, he
closes the chapter with a fervent exclamation as to the
beauty and goodness of Jehovah. His closing sentence is

[2]E. B. Pusey, *The Minor Prophets,* II, 411.

composed of poetic terms which speak of prosperity and
abundance (cf. Ps. 4:7).

BLESSING FOR JUDAH AND EPHRAIM (10:1-12)

In this chapter Israel's redemption and regathering
are further pictured. "Ask ye of the LORD rain in the
time of the latter rain; so the LORD shall make bright
clouds, and give them showers of rain, to everyone grass
in the field" (10:1). Israel is encouraged to ask blessing,
not from idols and false prophets who cannot really help,
but from Jehovah. They are urged to ask rain of the
Lord in the "time of the latter rain." *Latter rain* refers
to the necessary rains just before the time of harvest,
which are as important as the early rains. God had promised to supply this to His people. Undoubtedly an application can be made not only to the necessary blessing
of *literal* rain, but also to the various *refreshing blessings*
God's people need at His hand. Christ said: "Ask, and
it shall be given you; seek, and ye shall find; knock, and
it shall be opened unto you" (Matt. 7:7). While His
people are asking such blessings, God is preparing and
supplying them. He will "give them showers of rain"
(literally, "pouring rain").

> For the idols have spoken vanity, and the di-
> viners have seen a lie, and have told false dreams;
> they comfort in vain: therefore they went their
> way as a flock, they were troubled, because there
> was no shepherd (10:2).

The *idols* mentioned here are literally *teraphim*. The
teraphim were the household idols which were worshiped
and inquired of by some of the people. They are re-

ferred to in connection with Rachel and Laban (Gen. 31:19), and also on other occasions in the history of Israel (e.g., Judges 17:5; 18:14 ff.; Ezek. 21:21; I Sam. 15:23). The *diviners* were those who consulted idols in an attempt to predict the future. God's people, led by these false, evil teachers, wander astray like sheep without a shepherd.

> Mine anger was kindled against the shepherds,
> and I punished the goats: for the LORD of hosts
> hath visited his flock the house of Judah, and hath
> made them as his goodly horse in the battle (10:3).

God's anger is kindled against these false shepherds who have led the sheep in the wrong way. Evil rulers are spoken of here as "he goats." These Jehovah will visit in judgment, but Israel will He visit in blessing. Israel is said to have been made as "his goodly horse." Again the allusion is to the horse as an instrument of warfare. The entire expression speaks of the strength to be given them by God (as does 9:13).

"Out of him came forth the corner, out of him the nail, out of him the battle-bow, out of him every oppressor together" (10:4). The *him* here refers to Judah, which has just been mentioned in the previous verse. Out of Judah came forth the cornerstone. This is another reference to the Messiah as the *cornerstone* (cf. Isa. 28:16). Out of Judah also came the "nail." The *nail* is a symbol of security, and here typifies the Messiah (cf. Isa. 22:22-23). This great Messiah, who is to come from Judah, is also described as "the battlebow." This pictures Christ as a great warrior (see Rev. 19:11-16). The last expression—"out of him [Judah] every oppressor together"—is difficult to interpret. In line with other phrases in the verse it seems to refer still to the Messiah, and may possibly signify that all authority is centered in Him.

> And they shall be as mighty men, which tread down their enemies in the mire of the streets in the battle: and they shall fight, because the LORD is with them, and the riders on horses shall be confounded. And I will strengthen the house of Judah, and I will save the house of Joseph, and I will bring them again to place them; for I have mercy upon them: and they shall be as though I had not cast them off: for I am the LORD their God, and will hear them. And they of Ephraim shall be like a mighty man, and their heart shall rejoice as through wine: yea, their children shall see it, and be glad; their heart shall rejoice in the LORD. I will hiss for them, and gather them; for I have redeemed them: and they shall increase as they have increased (10:5-8).

God's people will be given victory over their enemies. All Israel is to be united once more in these future days of blessing, so both the northern and southern kingdoms are mentioned together in this passage. The power and joy of Ephraim (a tribal name sometimes used for Israel as a whole) in that day and the regathering of Israel from among the nations preparatory to the millennial blessings are depicted. God had previously said that He would summon their enemies against them by "hissing" (Isa. 7:18-19). Now in the same way He summons His people back to their own land. The statement that "they shall increase as they have increased" is likely a reference

to the multiplication of the children of Israel during
their sojourn in Egypt (see Exodus 1).

> And I will sow them among the people: and they
> shall remember me in far countries; and they shall
> live with their children, and turn again. I will
> bring them again also out of the land of Egypt,
> and gather them out of Assyria; and I will bring
> them into the land of Gilead and Lebanon; and
> place shall not be found for them (10:9-10).

These verses recapitulate the dispersion and regathering.
The dispersion is spoken of as a *sowing* by God. In their
dispersion they will finally remember and call upon
Jehovah, even as they did centuries ago in Egypt. When
they do, Jehovah shall surely answer and they "shall
live." Egypt and Assyria, the two former enemies of
Israel, are used typically of all the nations into which
Israel has been scattered, while Gilead and Lebanon
represent the entire land of Palestine. The land which
was desolate shall once again be filled with people.

> And he shall pass through the sea with affliction,
> and shall smite the waves in the sea, and all the
> deeps of the river shall dry up: and the pride of
> Assyria shall be brought down, and the scepter of
> Egypt shall depart away (10:11).

At the same time Israel is being regathered, their enemies
shall be punished. The sea smitten and the deeps of the
river drying up are without doubt references to Israel's
former deliverance from Egypt through the Red Sea. At
that time Israel was saved, and their enemies annihilated.

Once again shall God work in such a miraculous fashion
for His people.

"And I will strengthen them in the LORD; and they
shall walk up and down in his name, saith the LORD"
(10:12). The "them" which God will strengthen refers
to Israel. In His name shall they walk up and down—a
figure which speaks of the fact that in Him they are to
have their very existence.

THE TRUE SHEPHERD REJECTED FOR THE
FALSE SHEPHERD (11:1-17)

In this chapter an unusual picture is given of the
coming of the Messiah, the true Shepherd, and His rejection by Israel is foretold. This brings the wrath of
God upon the land, and paves the way for the coming of
the false shepherd, the Beast King of Daniel 7:8 and
Revelation 19:20—the Antichrist whose eventual destruction is also prophesied.

> Open thy doors, O Lebanon, that the fire may
> devour thy cedars. Howl, fir tree; for the cedar is
> fallen; because the mighty are spoiled: howl, O ye
> oaks of Bashan; for the forest of the vintage is
> come down. There is a voice of the howling of the
> shepherds; for their glory is spoiled: a voice of the
> roaring of young lions; for the pride of Jordan is
> spoiled (11:1-3).

This chapter opens with a picture of the *result* of the
wrath of God. Later the *cause* of that wrath is explained.
Lebanon is often used by the prophets as being descrip-
tive of the glory of Jerusalem (Isa. 14:8; 37:24; Jer.
22:6, 7; Ezek. 17:3, 12). This glory lay in the temple,

which was built in part from the cedars of Lebanon. Now the door is to be "opened" and the fire is to "devour"—a graphic scene of the destruction of Jerusalem.

The cedars, representing the leaders, have been destroyed, and the lower ones shall fall also. The shepherds wail because their pasture lands are gone, while the young lions, usually their enemies, join in their grief due to the desolation of the land. Typically speaking, these represent both the proud and humble people of the nation.

> Thus saith the LORD my God; Feed the flock of slaughter; whose possessors slay them, and hold themselves not guilty: and they that sell them say, Blessed be the Lord; for I am rich: and their own shepherds pity them not. For I will no more pity the inhabitants of the land, saith the Lord: but, lo, I will deliver the men every one into his neighbor's hand, and into the hand of his king: and they shall smite the land, and out of their hand I will not deliver them (11:4-6).

The "flock of slaughter" is Israel upon whom the wrath of God has come. They are "the flock of slaughter" because the Gentile nations destroying them do not feel they have done any wrong. Indeed their enemies count themselves as instruments of God. Those who should have been their leaders think only of themselves and not of the people. But most terrible of all is the statement that because they have rejected the true and followed false shepherds, Jehovah Himself shall no more pity them, but there will be both civil war within the land and destruction from without.

In the verses that now follow, a most astounding picture is painted of the rejection of Christ at His first coming. In this section Zechariah himself represents the true Shepherd to come. In this role he symbolically carries out certain actions that speak of the rejection of the Messiah, which is the cause of the wrath of God pictured in the preceding verses.

> And I will feed the flock of slaughter, even you,
> O poor of the flock. And I took unto me two
> staves; the one I called Beauty, and the other I
> called Bands; and I fed the flock (11:7).

The prophet, as representative of the Messiah—the Lord Jesus Christ—feeds the flock of Israel, especially "the poor of the flock." The latter expression probably refers to the godly who were poor through persecution of the wicked. Zechariah speaks of two staves which he had. Two staves were customarily used by the shepherd (cf. Ps. 23:4), one as a weapon against wild animals who would harm the flock, and one to guide the sheep. The two staves which Zechariah used have a symbolical meaning. The first is called *Beauty*. Other possible translations are *grace* or *favor*. This staff then speaks of God's *grace* in sending His Son, the Messiah, to Israel. The other staff is called *Bands* or "binders," signifying the unity intended by God for the entire nation.

"Three shepherds also I cut off in one month; and my soul loathed them, and their also soul abhorred me" (11:8). Who are these three shepherds that God cuts off? Some expositors identify these with certain individuals,[3]

[3]E.g. Hitzig. See C. H. H. Wright, *Zechariah and His Prophecies*, p. 318-19.

but most Bible students take them to be representative of three classes of leaders in Israel—prophets, priests, and kings[4] (cf. Jer. 2:8). All three of these classes of "shepherds" are to be cut off from Israel in a short and definitely settled period of time. The fulfillment is to be found in the destruction of Jerusalem by the Romans shortly after the rejection of the Messiah. This destruction was accomplished A.D. 70. The last part of the verse certainly pictures graphically the attitude of the Lord Jesus Christ toward these official leaders of Israel, and their attitude toward Him. The Shepherd says: "My soul loathed [or wearied] of them, and their soul also abhorred me." Remember how the leaders hated Him, and how they reviled Him during the crucifixion (Matt. 27:39-43).

"Then said I, I will not feed you: that that dieth, let it die; and that that is to be cut off, let it be cut off; and let the rest eat every one the flesh of another" (11:9). Here is a sad picture of the Shepherd turning away from the rebellious sheep. Complete confusion and destruction follow (cf. Matt. 23:37-39).

"And I took my staff, even Beauty, and cut it asunder, that I might break my covenant which I had made with all the people" (11:10). Israel is now abandoned to destruction as prophesied in verses 1-6. The staff called Beauty is now broken, so that the Shepherd may "break my covenant which I had made with all the people." What was this covenant? It was the covenant God had imposed upon all the nations to prevent their harming Israel. This is now broken.

"And it was broken in that day: and so the poor of the

4Jerome held this view. See Pusey, p. 424.

flock that waited upon me knew that it was the word of the LORD" (11:11). When these events of judgment take place then the poor but godly remnant of the flock recognize the hand of Jehovah in the destruction.

> And I said unto them, If ye think good, give me my price; and if not, forbear. So they weighed for my price thirty pieces of silver. And the LORD said unto me, Cast it unto the potter: a goodly price that I was prized at of them. And I took the thirty pieces of silver, and cast them to the potter in the house of the Lord (11:12-13).

The prophet, still representing the good Shepherd, asks the people of his "hire." In other words, they are to set a value upon his services to them. If they wish, they can place no value whatever. What do the people do? They contemptuously offer *thirty pieces of silver*. This was the price of a slave gored by an ox (Exodus 21:32). This is more insulting than no price at all. It is startling to notice that when Judas asked for a price to be placed on the head of Christ, "the high priest, knowingly or unknowingly, fixed on the price named by Zechariah."[5]

The price, contemptuously given, is cast aside with contempt (for *cast* as a gesture of contempt and disgust, see Exodus 22:31; Isa. 14:19; II Sam. 18:17; II Kings 23:12). The money is "cast to the potter." This expression is rather difficult to interpret, because later in the verse it is said that the shepherd casts it to the potter "in the house of the Lord." Some have thought that there was a pottery just outside the temple. Others have felt that the price was cast down in the temple and was then

[5]*Ibid*, p. 427.

given to the potter. A fulfillment is seen in the fact that Judas, the betrayer of Christ, cast his blood money down in the temple, and it was then used to purchase the "potter's field" in which to bury paupers (Matt. 27:3-10).

The sum of thirty pieces of silver the Shepherd calls "the goodly price that I was prized at of them." This is of course an expression of irony.

"Then I cut asunder mine other staff, even Bands, that I might break the brotherhood between Judah and Israel" (11:14). Now the other staff—*Bands,* or *binders* —is broken, signifying that the union of the nation is now broken, to be fully restored only in the millennial kingdom.

The good Shepherd rejected, the false shepherd now comes on the scene. "And the LORD said unto me, Take unto thee yet the instruments of a foolish shepherd" (11:15). Zechariah is now to symbolize another prophetic picture, this time by taking the equipment of a "foolish shepherd." This foolish shepherd is the Beast King of the last days, the "man of sin" of II Thessalonians 2:3-12. It should be remembered that in the Old Testament the "foolish" one is the one who turns from God and leaves Him out of his life (Ps. 14:1). "Folly" is an Old Testament expression for *sin* (see, e.g., Gen. 34:7; Deut. 22:21; Joshua 7:15; Judges 19:23, etc.).

> For, lo, I will raise up a shepherd in the land, which shall not visit those that be cut off, neither shall seek the young one, nor heal that that is broken, nor feed that that standeth still: but he

shall eat the flesh of the fat, and tear their claws
in pieces (11:16).

The false shepherd's true character is revealed. Instead
of feeding the sheep, it is said that "he shall eat the flesh
of the fat." He cares nothing for those in distress. He is,
however, raised up by the permissive will of God, in the
same way that the Assyrians and the Babylonians were
raised up to punish God's people.

> Woe to the idol shepherd that leaveth the flock!
> The sword shall be upon his arm, and upon his
> right eye: his arm shall be clean dried up, and his
> right eye shall be utterly darkened (11:17).

Judgment is pronounced upon the false shepherd, in
words strongly reminiscent of John 10:12-13. The false
shepherd's claim is to strength and intelligence, so the
judgment is directed against the *arm* and the *eye*, which
symbolize these features.

THE SIEGE OF JERUSALEM AND THE DELIVERANCE BY JEHOVAH (12:1-14)

In this chapter the final terrible siege of Jerusalem is
described. Also pictured are the deliverance of Jerusalem from the siege, and the kingdom blessing which
follows:

> The burden of the word of the LORD for Israel,
> saith the LORD, which stretcheth forth the heavens,
> and layeth the foundation of the earth, and form-
> eth the spirit of man within him (12:1).

Once again the term *burden* is used to signify a prophecy
of grief. Grief must come before blessing for Israel.

God's omnipotence is shown in order to give weight to
the prediction to follow.

"Behold, I will make Jerusalem a cup of trembling
unto all the people round about, when they shall be in
the siege both against Judah and against Jerusalem"
(12:2). The *cup* usually represents God's displeasure.
Jerusalem is to be a cup held by her enemies, trembling
with fear as they surround her. The siege is against
Judah, and also against Jerusalem, the capital of Judah.

> And in that day will I make Jerusalem a burden-
> some stone for all people: all that burden them-
> selves with it shall be cut in pieces, though all the
> people of the earth be gathered together against
> it (12:3).

Her enemies may surround and trouble her, but she will
prove to be a burden too heavy for them to bear. Those
who fight against Jerusalem will in the end be destroyed.

> In that day, saith the LORD, I will smite every
> horse with astonishment, and his rider with mad-
> ness: and I will open mine eyes upon the house of
> Judah, and will smite every horse of the people
> with blindness (12:4).

Horses once more are used to speak of warfare. All the
forces against Jerusalem are to be smitten with "astonish-
ment." God will turn yet again in mercy to Judah, as
He observes their distress.

> And the governors of Judah shall say in their
> heart, The inhabitants of Jerusalem shall be my
> strength in the LORD of hosts their God. In that
> day will I make the governors of Judah like an

> hearth of fire among the wood, and like a torch of
> fire in a sheaf; and they shall devour all the people
> round about, on the right hand and on the left:
> and Jerusalem shall be inhabited again in her own
> place, even in Jerusalem (12:5-6) .

In that day the leaders shall find in the people of Jerusalem their strength, in Jehovah. A picture is sketched
of the fire that will come from Judah to consume their
enemies. They are to be like a torch of fire in a sheaf.
After the battle is completed, there is to be peace for
Jerusalem.

> The LORD also shall save the tents of Judah first,
> that the glory of the house of David and the glory
> of the inhabitants of Jerusalem do not magnify
> themselves against Judah. In that day shall the
> Lord defend the inhabitants of Jerusalem: and he
> that is feeble among them at that day shall be as
> David; and the house of David shall be as God,
> as the angel of the LORD before them (12:7-8) .

The defenseless portions are to be saved first, so that the
hand of Jehovah may be clearly seen, and that no man
may glory. The Lord Jehovah is Jerusalem's real defense, and in that day of His deliverance even the weak
and stumbling in Israel shall be like David, the great
king of Israel who fell but was raised again. Further
"the house of David shall be as God." Clearly this is a
reference to that great Son of David, the Lord Jesus
Christ, who is both Man and God—Immanuel, "God
with us."

"And it shall come to pass in that day, that I will seek
to destroy all the nations that come against Jerusalem"

(12:9). Woe is pronounced on the enemies who have surrounded Jerusalem. God always accomplishes that which He "seeks"—in tis instance it is their destruction.

> And I will pour upon the house of David, and upon the inhabitants of Jerusalem, the spirit of grace and of supplications: and they shall look upon me whom they have pierced, and they shall mourn for him, as one mourneth for his only son, and shall be in bitterness for him, as one that is in bitterness for his first-born (12:10).

This great verse speaks of a future outpouring of the Holy Spirit upon Jerusalem. He is the Spirit of God's "grace" and also of "supplications," as the repentant people seek this grace. Now at last they look *upon* (or better, *unto* as in the ASV) their rejected Messiah whom they have pierced. This Hebrew word translated *pierced* is everywhere used in the sense of "thrust through"[6] and surely indicates the death of the Messiah.

Then comes national repentance as they realize what they have really done in rejecting their Messiah. A divine preview of this is to be seen in the case of Saul of Tarsus, the one to whom the risen Christ appeared as to "one born out of due time" (I Cor. 15:8; the Greek here clearly means *before* the appointed time). The bitterness of this mourning of Israel is described, when it is said to resemble the mourning for an only son, or for a first-born son. This is the same deliverance pictured in Romans 11:25-27.

"In that day shall there be a great mourning in Jerusalem, as the mourning of Hadadrimmon in the valley

[6]And so translated in Num. 25:8; Judges 9:54; I Sam. 31:4; I Chron. 10:4; Zech. 13:3.

of Megiddon" (12:11). The mourning is further described as being like "the mourning of Hadadrimmon in the valley of Megiddon," apparently a reference to the place where the good King Josiah of Judah was slain by Pharaoh Necho, which occasioned much mourning (II Chron. 35:20-27).

> And the land shall mourn, every family apart; the family of the house of David apart, and their wives apart; the family of the house of Nathan apart, and their wives apart; the family of the house of Levi apart, and their wives apart; the family of Shimei apart, and their wives apart; all the families that remain, every family apart, and their wives apart (12:12-14).

Mourning in individual families, as well as national mourning, takes place. The "family of the house of David" is mentioned as mourning apart. The reference is to David's descendants through the regal line of Solomon, from which Joseph the husband of Mary was descended (Matt. 1:16). Also the "family of the house of Nathan" shall mourn. Nathan was a brother of Solomon, through whom Mary was descended (Luke 3:31). The family of Levi and that of Shimei are priestly families, and speak of the priesthood (Num. 3:21). After these four families are mentioned by name, it is finally said that "all the families" participate in this bitter mourning.

> But though these, as the two aristocratic and privileged lines, the rulers and priests, who alas! in times past often set an *evil* example to the whole nation, will now be foremost in their self-contrition and mourning over the great national sin, their

> example for *good* will now also be followed by all
> the rest of the people. This is expressed in the
> last verse of the chapter, which tells us that "all the
> families that remain shall mourn, every family
> apart, and their wives apart."[7]

All the families are specified as mourning *apart* from
one another. Even husbands and wives mourn apart
from each other. This certainly indicates a great *individual* sorrow as each one realizes his *individual* part
in the rejection and crucifixion of the Messiah. It is indeed no mere outward formality that is here referred to,
such as the Lord previously reprimanded. It is a true
contrition of heart and a real turning to the Lord. In a
beautiful beatitude, Jesus Christ said: "Blessed are they
that mourn: for they shall be comforted" (Matt. 5:4).
When this real contrition of heart comes, then the Lord
Himself will comfort the hearts of the people of Israel.
Then, as the very next verse (13:1) tells us: "There shall
be a fountain opened to the house of David and to the inhabitants of Jerusalem for sin and for uncleanness."

Christians should look forward with great expectancy
toward this great day of national mourning and blessing
yet to come for Israel. Meantime, it must not be forgotten that any individual, whether Jew or Gentile, may
even now receive such blessing by looking unto the
pierced One—the Messiah who has *already* come—the
Lord Jesus Christ who "died for our sins according to the
scriptures." If you have never done so before, will you
not do it now? Look at Jesus, dying for *your* sins there
on the cross of Calvary. Look with the eye of faith at

[7]Baron, p. 453.

Him rising from the dead to be *your* living Saviour. "If thou shalt confess with thy mouth the Lord Jesus, and shalt believe in thine heart that God hath raised him from the dead, thou shalt be saved" (Rom. 10:9).

THE CLEANSING OF ISRAEL (13:1-6)

In this great chapter Zechariah gives a further picture of the time when the wonderful prophecy of 12:10 shall be fulfilled. When God's Holy Spirit deals in marvelous convicting power with Israel, then they shall look unto Him whom they have pierced—the Lord Jesus Christ their Messiah—and shall mourn for their past error of rejecting Him. *When* they do this, *then* the fountain for cleansing is revealed. The chapter in addition goes on to foretell the complete cessation of idolatry and false prophecy among the Israelites in that day.

"In that day there shall be a fountain opened to the house of David and to the inhabitants of Jerusalem for sin and for uncleanness" (13:1). In his last three chapters Zechariah uses the expression "in that day" no less than thirteen times to refer to this future time of judgment and of blessing. When God's ancient people receive Him whom they once rejected (Jer. 2:15; 17:13), then in that future day "there shall be a fountain opened." The primary purpose of this fountain is not *refreshment* but *cleansing*. It is not just to quench thirst, but to cleanse from the defilement of sin. That is what all men need more than anything else. Solomon, the wisest man, as he dedicated the temple, expressed a sad but important truth: "There is no man that sinneth not" (I Kings 8:46). King David, the sweet psalmist of

Israel, uttered the same truth: "The Lord looked down from heaven upon the children of men, to see if there were any that did understand, and seek God. They are all gone aside, they are all together become filthy: there is none that doeth good, no, not one" (Ps. 14:2, 3). The apostle Paul refers to these words of the psalmist in Romans 3, and reiterates the teaching when he writes: "All have sinned and come short of the glory of God" (Rom. 3:23).

So *all* need cleansing from the *defilement* of sin. Thank God that such a fountain of cleansing has been provided in the atonement wrought by Jesus Christ on the cross, when He "bore our sins in his own body on the tree" (I Peter 2:24). The writer of Hebrews affirms that Jesus Christ "procured man's purification from sins" (1:3, Williams' translation). This cleansing is available even now to any individual either of Israel or of the Gentile nations who will look in faith unto the pierced One. "Believe on the Lord Jesus Christ, and thou shalt be saved" (Acts 16:31).

> And it shall come to pass in that day, saith the Lord of hosts, that I will cut off the names of the idols out of the land, and they shall no more be remembered: and also I will cause the prophets and the unclean spirit to pass out of the land (13:2).

In that day of repentance not only is idol worship to be destroyed, but even the names of the idols will be "cut off" so that they will be utterly forgotten. The false prophets shall be done away with, and also the unclean spirits which moved them.

> And it shall come to pass, that when any shall
> yet prophesy, then his father and his mother that
> begat him shall say unto him, Thou shalt not live;
> for thou speakest lies in the name of the LORD:
> and his father and his mother that begat him shall
> thrust him through when he prophesieth (13:3).

A hypothetical case is here cited to show what *would*
happen should any still dare in that day to act as a false
prophet. Even his own parents, because of their rever-
ence for Jehovah, would turn against him and "thrust
him through." This is in accordance with the precept in
Deuteronomy 13:6-10.

> And it shall come to pass in that day, that the
> prophets shall be ashamed every one of his vision,
> when he hath prophesied; neither shall they wear a
> rough garment to deceive: but he shall say, I am no
> prophet, I am an husbandman; for man taught me
> to keep cattle from my youth (13:4-5).

Those who before were false prophets shall now be
ashamed of themselves. No more shall they wear the
hairy garment, indicative of a true prophet such as Elijah
or John the Baptist, in order to deceive those who look
upon the outward appearance only. And, if inquiry is
made, the one who was formerly a false prophet, or who
is suspected, shall roundly deny that he is a prophet. Instead of claiming the high office of a prophet, he will
claim only the lowliest—that of a husbandman (farmer),
and that, further, from his youth.

"And one shall say unto him, What are these wounds
in thine hands? Then he shall answer, Those with which
I was wounded in the house of my friends" (13:6). This

is a somewhat difficult statement to interpret. Many
Bible teachers connect this with the verse that immediately follows it and thus take it to be a Messianic prophecy similar to Zechariah 12:10.[8] However from the context it seems to be a further questioning of the false
prophet, mentioned in the verse just preceding. The expression "in thine hands" is literally "between thine
hands,"[9] signifying wounds on the breast. Such terminol-
ogy would hardly be used of the wounds inflicted on
Christ at the crucifixion. The man being questioned has
denied that he ever was a false prophet. His questioner,
however, is suspicious and persists in the examination. It
was customary for false prophets to inflict cuttings or
wounds on themselves (see I Kings 18:28; Jer. 16:6, etc.).
So the suspect is asked to explain the wounds or scars
which he has on his body. He has an answer: "Those
with which I was wounded in the house of my friends."
Thus he attributes them to chastisement received perhaps as a boy in the house of relatives.

SCATTERING OF ISRAEL AFTER THE SHEPHERD IS SMITTEN (13:7-9)

The prophet now gives a brief résumé of the condition
of Israel throughout the age from the smiting of their
Shepherd at Calvary until the time when they are
cleansed and prepared for the kingdom.

> Awake, O sword, against my shepherd, and
> against the man that is my fellow, saith the LORD
> of hosts: smite the shepherd, and the sheep shall

[8]E.g. Pusey, p. 444.
[9]ASV reads "between thy arms" and notes in the margin "Heb. *hands*."

> be scattered: and I will turn mine hand upon the
> little ones (13:7).

The language is highly poetic. The sword, representing
death, is personified and commanded to smite Jehovah's
Shepherd, the *true* Shepherd. Though the people were
guilty of doing this deed themselves, yet at the same
time it was done through the divine will of God and
thus was the means by which redemption was accomplished (cf. Isa. 53:10; Acts 2:23). This smitten Shepherd is described as "the man that is my fellow, saith
Jehovah of hosts." Thus He is placed on an equality
with Jehovah, a clear indication of the Trinity.

With their Shepherd rejected, the sheep have no one
to guide them and therefore go astray—a picture of Israel
during the present age. "I will turn my hand"—who is
the "I" here? It is Jehovah, who will turn His hand in
judgment. When did this scattering take place? Primarily at the destruction of Jerusalem by Titus in A.D.
70. Since that time Israel has been scattered over all the
earth. In Matthew 26:31-32 our Lord alludes to this
very verse from Zechariah, and a special application is
made to the disciples being scattered. But this was only
a prefigure of the greater scattering of the entire nation
which was soon to come. That this is the fuller significance is made clear by the very next verse.

"And it shall come to pass, that in all the land, saith
the LORD, two parts therein shall be cut off and die; but
the third shall be left therein" (13:8). A large number
of Israel, spoken of here as two-thirds, is to be cut off.
When Titus destroyed Jerusalem 1,500,000 Jews died by
sword, pestilence, and famine. During the last days it

is evident that a similar judgment will take place, and
only a remnant will survive this judgment to enter the
kingdom (Ezek. 20:33-44).

> And I will bring the third part through the fire,
> and will refine them as silver is refined, and will try
> them as gold is tried: they shall call on my name,
> and I will hear them: I will say, It is my people:
> and they shall say, The LORD is my God (13:9).

Only a remnant of one-third of the nation remains and
this third part is only to be saved after having been
severely tried. The symbol of refining precious metals is
used to illustrate this trial. With this remnant the covenant relationship shall be restored.

> Two-thirds may be "cut off" and die, but the
> nation can never be *utterly* destroyed. There is
> always "a third," or "a tenth," which forms the
> indestructible "holy seed," which God takes care
> to preserve as the nucleus of the great and blessed
> nation through whom His holy will and His won-
> derful purposes in relation to this earth shall yet
> be realized. "I will make a full end," He says,
> "of all nations whither I have scattered thee, but I
> will not make a full end of thee."
>
> Hence no fires of tribulation, however hot, have
> been able utterly to consume them; and no waters
> of affliction, however deep, to drown them.
>
> And the end of the Lord in all the chastisements
> and judgments with which He has to visit His
> people on account of their great and manifold
> sins, is not their destruction, but that they may,
> by these very judgments, as well as by the abundant
> mercy which He will reveal to them "in that day,"

be brought as a nation *fully, and forever,* to know Him, in all the divine perfections of His glorious character, so as to be able to fulfill their foreordained mission to show forth His praise, and to proclaim His glory among the nations.[10]

THE COMING OF THE KING AND THE KINGDOM
(14:1-21)

The final chapter of Zechariah reveals further events concerning the siege of Jerusalem, which is to take place in the last days. It also pictures the deliverance of Israel through the coming of their great King, who then sets up His kingdom on earth. All this is to take place at the second coming of Christ. In addition the chapter depicts the millennial kingdom over which He will reign.

The last three verses of chapter 13 contain a prophecy of the cutting off of the true Shepherd of Israel (the Messiah at His first coming). This smiting of the Shepherd was to be followed by the scattering of the sheep. During this scattering, or dispersion, many will be "cut off." Only a remnant will remain and these will pass through the fire. This prophecy pictures Israel throughout all the present age, but especially looks forward to the great tribulation of the last days—to "the time of Jacob's trouble." A previous chapter (12) presented a prophetic picture of a great siege of Jerusalem which is to take place during these tribulation days. Now in the opening part of chapter 14 the prophecy returns to the time of this great siege, and reveals the wonderful deliverance God will bring about for His people. The picture is as vivid as if the writer were describing an actual

[10]Baron, p. 485.

historic event which had taken place already and had
been witnessed by him. But, after all, remember that
divine prophecy is just history written in advance.

In David Baron's great volume on Zechariah, these
words appear in the third edition, printed in 1919:

> First of all we have to suppose a restoration of
> the Jews in a condition of unbelief—not a complete
> restoration of the whole nation, which will not
> take place till after their conversion, but of a rep-
> resentative and influential remnant. It seems from
> Scripture that in relation to Israel and the land
> there will be a restoration, before the second advent
> of our Lord, of very much the same state of things
> as existed at the time of His first advent when the
> threads of God's dealing with them nationally were
> finally dropped, not to be taken up again "until the
> times of the Gentiles shall be fulfilled."
>
> There was at that time a number of Jews in
> Palestine representative of the nation; but com-
> pared with the number of their brethren, who were
> already a diaspora among the nations, they were a
> mere minority, and not in a politically independent
> condition.
>
> So it will be again. There will be at first, as com-
> pared with the whole nation, only a representative
> minority in Palestine, and a Jewish state will be
> probably formed, either under the suzerainty of
> one of the Great Powers, or under international
> protection.
>
> . . . But what follows? After a brief interval of
> prosperity there comes a night of anguish. What
> occasions the darkest hour in the night of Israel's

sad history since their rejection of Christ is the gathering of the nations and the siege predicted in this chapter.[11]

In 1948 the State of Israel was created, occupying territory designated by the United Nations. This was just such a consummation as predicted by Baron in the above quotation. How could he make such an uncanny prophecy? Simply because he was a student of the prophetic Scriptures and knew that "what he [God] had promised, he was able also to perform." All these facts should be kept in mind as one approaches the opening verses of Zechariah 14.

"Behold, the day of the LORD cometh, and thy spoil shall be divided in the midst of thee" (14:1). Now has arrived the "day of the LORD." This is the day "in which He Himself shall be Judge, and no longer leave man to fulfill his own will, and despise God's; in which His glory and holiness and the righteousness of His ways shall be revealed."[12]

> For I will gather all nations against Jerusalem to battle, and the city shall be taken, and the houses rifled, and the women ravished; and half the city shall go forth into captivity, and the residue of the people shall not be cut off from the city (14:2).

By connecting various prophecies concerning the last days (such as those of Daniel), we learn that a terrible Beast King (or Antichrist) shall arise in that period. He will make a seven-year covenant with this State of Israel. But in the midst of this seven-year period (the

[11]*Ibid.*, pp. 492-93.
[12]Pusey, pp. 448-49.

"seventieth week" of Dan. 9), this great king breaks his
covenant, requires worship for himself and, when the
people of Israel refuse, comes down upon them to exter-
minate them. This leads to the great siege of Jerusalem.

It is evident from the verses just referred to above that
the siege is in the beginning successful, for it is said that
the spoil of the city is divided in the midst of her. In
addition there take place scenes of horror and brutality
such as usually accompany the fall of a city into the hands
of an angry enemy. "Half the city" is taken into captivity. However it is surprisingly stated that the balance
"shall not be cut off from the city." This undoubtedly
proves that the siege here described could not have already taken place, because this description does not fit
any past overthrow of Jerusalem.

"Then shall the LORD go forth, and fight against those
nations, as when he fought in the day of battle" (14:3).
Just at this time of Israel's greatest need, deliverance
comes—not from man but from the Lord Jehovah. The
Lord Himself is coming down from heaven to fight
against those nations "as when he fought in the day of
battle." The expression refers not to some particular
event but to any occasion in which He might fight, when
His mighty power would be demonstrated.

> And his feet shall stand in that day upon the
> mount of Olives, which is before Jerusalem on the
> east, and the mount of Olives shall cleave in the
> midst thereof toward the east and toward the west,
> and there shall be a very great valley; and half of
> the mountain shall remove toward the north, and
> half of it toward the south (14:4).

Now it can be seen that this great Deliverer is none other than the Messiah who once came to earth and then returned to heaven again: Jehovah-Jesus. Upon exactly the same spot from which He ascended to heaven, there He will return (Luke 24:50, 51; Acts 1:9-12). The Mount of Olives is the highest peak in a line of hills overhanging Jerusalem, and rises several hundred feet above the city. When the Messiah—the Lord Jesus Christ—returns to this spot, an unusual natural phenomenon takes place. The mount is split from east to west, forming a great valley. This prediction proves that these events have not yet taken place.

> And ye shall flee to the valley of the mountains; for the valley of the mountains shall reach unto Azal: yea, ye shall flee, like as ye fled from before the earthquake in the days of Uzziah king of Judah: and the LORD my God shall come, and all the saints with thee (14:5).

The "ye" in this verse refers to the inhabitants of Jerusalem. They shall flee by the way of the valley which has just been made by the splitting of the Mount of Olives. The valley is said to reach unto "Azal." Azal has not been conclusively identified, but is probably the same as Beth-Ezel (Micah 1:11). This flight is compared with that which occurred during the reign of Uzziah (Amos 1:1). That past flight must indeed have been of large proportions to have been remembered for so long a time.

Most glorious of all are the words "the LORD my God shall come." Jehovah will come in the Person of the once-rejected Messiah. In the vividness of the prophecy, Zechariah suddenly uses direct discourse, when he com-

ments, "all the saints with thee." The term *saints* or
holy ones probably here refers to the risen human saints,
though it may conceivably also include the holy angels.

"And it shall come to pass in that day, that the light
shall not be clear, nor dark" (14:16). This verse is plain-
er in the American Standard Version: "And it shall come
to pass in that day, that there shall not be light; the
bright ones shall withdraw themselves." Natural light
is to be abated in that day. A phenomenon takes place
with regard to the stars ("the bright ones"). They are
said to "contract" or "congeal."

"But it shall be one day which shall be known to the
LORD, not day, nor night: but it shall come to pass, that
at evening time it shall be light" (14:7). This will be
one special day different from any other day—a day which
Jehovah alone knows and understands in all its fullness.
With the natural light abated, this particular day shall
be neither day nor night, as man understands such terms.
At the time when darkness ordinarily sets in, there shall
be light of a divine nature.

> And it shall be in that day, that living waters
> shall go out from Jerusalem; half of them toward
> the former sea, and half of them toward the hinder
> sea: in summer and in winter shall it be (14:8).

This great prophecy is in line with Joel 3:18; Ezekiel
47:2; and Revelation 22:1-2. "Living waters" come
forth from Jerusalem for the "healing of the nations."
Half of these waters flow into the Eastern (or Dead) Sea,
and half into the Western (or Mediterranean) Sea. The
waters flow unabated in both summer and winter, the
seasons having no effect upon them.

"And the LORD shall be king over all the earth: in that day shall there be one LORD, and his name one" (14:9). This speaks of the universal kingdom of Jehovah. He has always been "one . . . and his name one," but these facts shall now be recognized by all.

> All the land shall be turned as a plain from Geba to Rimmon south of Jerusalem: and it shall be lifted up, and inhabited in her place, from Benjamin's gate unto the place of the first gate, unto the corner gate, and from the tower of Hananeel unto the king's winepresses (14:10).

The mountains around Jerusalem are to be lowered so that all the land will become "like the Arabah"[13] (ASV), the largest plain of Judea. Thus Jerusalem will stand out above all the rest of the countryside. The ancient site of the city is described to show that it has been rebuilt in all of its former splendor.

"And men shall dwell in it, and there shall be no more utter destruction; but Jerusalem shall be safely inhabited" (14:11). Once again it is fully inhabited. The curse which came because of sin is removed. There is no fear of any further attack.

> And this shall be the plague wherewith the LORD will smite all the people that have fought against Jerusalem; their flesh shall consume away while they stand upon their feet, and their eyes shall consume away in their holes, and their tongue shall consume away in their mouth (14:12).

[13]"Term frequently used in Old Testament for the Jordan Valley (Deut. 1:7; 3:17; Joshua 11:2), and variously translated as 'plain,' 'plains,' 'desert,' 'valley,' or 'wilderness.'". Charles F. Pfeiffer, *Baker's Bible Atlas*, p. 286.

More detail is now given concerning the destruction of
the enemies who were besieging Jerusalem. It is to be,
first of all, a destruction through the action of Jehovah.
God's enemies are to be consumed even while they stand
prepared to resist.

> And it shall come to pass in that day, that a great
> tumult from the LORD shall be among them; and
> they shall lay hold every one on the hand of his
> neighbor, and his hand shall rise up against the
> hand of his neighbor (14:13).

Even as He did in Old Testament times, Jehovah will
also send confusion among these armies, and they will
fight against each other (cf. Judges 7:22; I Sam. 14:20).

"And Judah also shall fight at Jerusalem; and the
wealth of all the heathen round about shall be gathered
together, gold, and silver, and apparel, in great abundance" (14:14). Besides the plague and confusion
among these wicked ones, the Israelites also shall fight
against them. Much spoil—gold, silver, and apparel—is
to be taken by Judah.

"And so shall be the plague of the horse, of the mule,
of the camel, and of the ass, and of all the beasts that
shall be in these tents, as this plague" (14:15). The beasts
of the enemy armies will suffer the same plague, as being
identified with the wickedness of their masters. All of
creation suffers because of the sin of man (Rom. 8:22).

> And it shall come to pass, that everyone that is
> left of all the nations which came against Jerusalem
> shall even go up from year to year to worship the

> King, the LORD of hosts, and to keep the feast of
> tabernacles (14:16).

A remnant of the nations is to remain to share the blessings of the millennium, despite this rebellion against
God. Instead of coming up against Jerusalem in war,
they now come to worship "from year to year." They
also come to celebrate the feast which spoke of millennial
blessing—the Feast of Tabernacles (Lev. 23:41-43).

"And it shall be, that whoso will not come up of all the
families of the earth unto Jerusalem to worship the King,
the LORD of hosts, even upon them shall be no rain"
(14:17). Apparently representatives of the various nations are to go up each year to attend this feast. The
nation which does not send such a representation is to be
punished by having rain withheld from their land. Rain
is essential to the well-being of any country, and is
spoken of as a blessing from God (Deut. 11:10-15). No
doubt there is also a spiritual application of blessing
withheld and of the consequent drying up of spiritual
life in such countries.

> And if the family of Egypt go not up, and come
> not, that have no rain; there shall be the plague,
> wherewith the Lord will smite the heathen that
> come not up to keep the feast of tabernacles
> (14:18).

Egypt is mentioned as a specific illustration of what will
happen to such a country, probably because that nation
depends on the Nile River for water and irrigation
rather than on seasonal rains.

"This shall be the punishment of Egypt, and the

punishment of all nations that come not up to keep the feast of tabernacles" (14:19). Even a country considering itself above the need of rain will suffer severely.

"In that day shall there be upon the bells of the horses, HOLINESS UNTO THE LORD; and the pots in the LORD's house shall be like the bowls before the altar" (14:20). Things completely secular in nature, such as "the bells of the horses," shall have upon them the same inscription that was once on the high priest's headdress: Holy to Jehovah (Exodus 39:30). This indicates the complete sanctification of all things. The humblest vessels in the temple will be considered as holy as the bowls which caught the blood of the sacrifices.

> Yea, every pot in Jerusalem and in Judah shall be holiness unto the LORD of hosts: and all they that sacrifice shall come and take of them, and seethe therein: and in that day there shall be no more the Canaanite in the house of the LORD of hosts (14:21).

Furthermore, every pot in the entire city and country will be holy. Flesh offered in sacrifices will be cooked in them since all are holy. No more shall there be "the Canaanite in the house of the LORD." The Canaanites were the sinful inhabitants of Palestine whom the Lord Jehovah judged. They were altogether evil and so not fit to be present in the house of Jehovah. How wonderful this holy kingdom which is to be ushered in by the coming of the great King, the Lord Jesus Christ! "Even so, come, Lord Jesus"!

BIBLIOGRAPHY

Baron, David. *The Visions and Prophecies of Zechariah*. London: Heb. Chr. Testimony to Israel, 1951.

Biederwolf, William Edward. *The Millennium Bible*. Grand Rapids: Baker, 1964.

Gaebelein, A. C. *The Angels of God*. New York: Our Hope, 1924.

———. *The Annotated Bible*. Vol. V, *Daniel-Malachi*. New York: Loizeaux, n.d.

Henry, Matthew. *Matthew Henry's Commentary on the Whole Bible*. Vol. IV, *Isaiah to Malachi*. New York: Revell, n.d.

Ironside, H. A. *Lectures on the Book of Revelation*. New York: Loizeaux, 1930.

———. *Notes on the Minor Prophets*. New York: Loizeaux, n.d.

Jamieson, Robert; Fausset, A. R.; and Brown, David. *A Commentary on the Old and New Testaments*. Grand Rapids: Eerdmans, 1948.

Keil, C. F. and Delitzsch, Franz. *Biblical Commentary on the Old Testament*. Vol. II, *The Twelve Minor Prophets*. Grand Rapids: Eerdmans, 1951.

Morgan, G. Campbell. *Living Messages of the Books of the Bible*. New York: Revell, 1912.

Pfeiffer, Charles F. *Baker's Bible Atlas*. Grand Rapids: Baker, 1961.

Pusey, E. B. *The Minor Prophets*. Vol. II. Grand Rapids: Baker, 1950.

Reich, Max. *The Messianic Hope of Israel.* Chicago: Moody, 1945.

Schaff, Philip (ed.). *Lange's Commentary.* Vol. XIV, *The Minor Prophets.* New York: Scribner's, 1915.

Scofield, C. I. The Scofield Reference Bible. New York: Oxford U., 1945.

Spence, H.D.M., and Exell, Joseph S. (eds.). *Pulpit Commentary.* Vol. XIV, *The Book of Zechariah.* Grand Rapids: Eerdmans, 1950.

Unger, Merrill F. *Unger's Bible Dictionary.* Chicago: Moody, 1957.

Walvoord, John F. *The Revelation of Jesus Christ.* Chicago: Moody, 1966.

Wright, Charles Henry Hamilton. *Zechariah and His Prophecies.* London: Hodder & Stoughton, 1879.

Young, Robert. *Analytical Concordance to the Bible.* New York: Funk & Wagnalls, n.d.